Raspberry Pi IoT In Python
Using GPIO Zero

Second Edition

Harry Fairhead & Mike James

I/O Press
I Programmer Library

Harry Fairhead & Mike James,
Raspberry Pi IoT In Python Using GPIO Zero
ISBN Paperback: 9781871962871
ISBN Hardback: 9781871962192
Second Edition
First Printing, February 2024
Revision 0

Published by IO Press   www.iopress.info
In association with I Programmer   www.i-programmer.info
and with I o T Programmer   www.iot-programmer.com

The publisher recognizes and respects all marks used by companies and manufacturers as a means to distinguish their products. All brand names and product names mentioned in this book are trade marks or service marks of their respective companies and our omission of trade marks is not an attempt to infringe on the property of others.

In particular we acknowledge that Raspberry Pi is a registered trademark of the Raspberry Pi Foundation.

Preface

The Raspberry Pi family is an attractive set of devices to use to learn about physical computing or the IoT, but what language to use? You can do some IoT development in Scratch and C is powerful, but there is nothing much easier than Python – especially if you already know Python. Add to this the fact that there is a library, GPIO Zero, which makes working with GPIO lines and more sophisticated devices easy, and you can see that it is an even better choice.

What is new is that with the Pi 5 none of the existing libraries in other languages work as it is not compatible with previous Pis. This makes GPIO Zero the only easy way to write IoT programs that work on all versions of the Pi including the Pi 5. It is the recommended way to work with the Pi 5 and hence even more attractive to use with all Pis.

The only downside of using Python is that it can be too slow for some IoT applications and in this case you really do need C. However, Python is plenty fast enough for projects that involve actions on the tens of millisecond scale and, given how easy it is to perform sophisticated data processing in these situations, it often has the edge.

This book is about using and understanding the hardware and GPIO Zero. It not only shows you how to "follow the beaten track", but how to create your own tracks. It isn't a project book, but many of the devices described are part way to projects and all of the devices and techniques described can be used to create practical projects.

The emphasis here is on understanding how things work and using this knowledge to create and work with new devices and integrate them into GPIO Zero.

You can use any Python development system that you know, but we describe how to use Thonny and VS Code to do remote development. If you do decide to use this method the time to get started is slightly greater, but it has a lot of advantages. In particular, you can keep your Python program on a main machine and run them on any Pi you can SSH into. This makes it very easy to try your programs out on different models of the Pi.

We would like to thank Sue Gee and Kay Ewbank for presiding as technical editors and making sure we kept our commas in line as well as being technically correct. Any errors that do remain are owned equally by both authors.

Harry Fairhead and Mike James

February 2024

3

For updates, errata, links to resources and the source code for the programs in this book visit its dedicated page on the IO Press website: www.iopress.info.

Table of Contents

Chapter 5
Simple On/Off Devices   **55**

Chapter 6
Pins And Pin Factories   **65**

Chapter 7
Some Electronics   **75**

Chapter 8
Simple Input   **93**

Chapter 9
Complex Input Devices   **109**

Chapter 10
Pulse Width Modulation   **131**

Chapter 11
Controlling Motors And Servos   **149**

Chapter 12
Working With Compound Devices   **175**

Chapter 13
The SPI Bus   **197**

Chapter 14
Custom SPI Devices   **207**

Chapter 15
Using The Lgpio Library

Appendix I
VS Code

Chapter 1

Why Pi For IoT?

The Raspberry Pi is a different sort of IoT computer. It isn't a small, cheap, but not-very-powerful, device – it is a cheap, but **more** powerful device. Running a full version of Linux and being supported by many different languages, it means that we are no longer restricted to assembler or C. Of the many higher-level languages available, Python is probably the most popular.

The whole idea of writing IoT-style programs in Python is relatively new and it has its advantages and disadvantages. Python is slow to react, but powerful when roused. It takes time to do simple things like notice that a button has been pressed, but it makes implementing complex algorithms easier.

This really is a new approach to the IoT and the Raspberry Pi is ideal for the task.

In this short chapter, we will take a look at the range of devices that are available in the Pi family and the reasons for selecting one rather than another to do particular jobs. The term IoT - Internet of Things - has become very popular and tends to be used in place of older terms such as embedded processing, micro-controllers and newer terms such as physical computing. The ideas, however, are related and in the rest of this book the term IoT will be used to mean a system being used to interface with the real world, usually via custom electronics, even if the Internet isn't explicitly involved.

The Raspberry Pi Or A Microcontroller?

Compared to the Pi, the Arduino and any similar microcontroller is a very low-powered computer. The basic Arduino isn't capable of running Linux, which is a full operating system. It simply runs the one program you have written for it. However, the Arduino and similar devices have a big advantage – they have dedicated, usually analog, I/O lines. The Pi doesn't have the same variety of I/O lines, but it has enough for many jobs and it can be easily expanded with the use of standard expansion boards called HATs (Hardware Attached on Top) because of the way they plug in. Some HATs are so commonly used that they are considered more or less standard and have their own Linux drivers.

To make the difference plain, you can use a Pi for almost any job that a desktop computer can do, including any server role. An Arduino, on the other hand, isn't up to this sort of work. Sometimes the fact that the Pi is a full computer makes it even more suitable for low-level jobs. For example, you want a new door bell? Why not use a Pi and have it say hello using a voice synthesizer.

In short, the Pi gives you more computing power for less money.

Everything isn't perfect with the Pi and the IoT. In particular, the use of Linux means that you can no longer pretend your program is the only program running. Linux is a multitasking operating system and it can suspend any program at any time to give another program a chance to run. If you are familiar with microcontroller programming then it will come as something of a shock that you do not have complete control of the machine. What is more, Linux isn't the easiest operating system to get to grips with if you are a beginner.

All of these problems and more can be overcome with a little work and it is worthwhile. The Pi is a fast and capable IoT computer and would still be a good choice even if it cost a lot more. We are entering a new era of embedded computing when the device that runs your washing machine is as powerful as your desktop computer.

Which Raspberry Pi?

The Raspberry Pi family has grown over the years and it can be difficult to keep track of the differences between the models. As far as the IoT goes, while you can use an early Pi 1 or Pi 2, it is much better not to. The modern range of devices is more powerful and if you are starting a new project it is better to use one of the current models. This said, the very latest Pi 5 is more expensive than the Pi 4, which is in turn more expensive than the Pi 3 and they are all currently available. They are also available with different amounts of memory and this is not something you can upgrade without a soldering iron and plenty of skill – and not recommended even then.

Cost rather than computing power can be an issue in an IoT project and while you cannot completely write off earlier models if you have them on hand, the Pi Zero range is low-cost. The later models

All this makes choosing a Pi difficult. My best advice is to use the fastest and most powerful Pi you can for development and when you have something working see what computing power is actually needed before deploying the finished program.

Pi Zero Range

The smallest in the Raspberry Pi family, and the cheapest at $10, is the Pi Zero which is about half as fast as a Pi 3, ten times slower than the Pi 4 and twenty times slower than the Pi 5. Even though it isn't as powerful, it is often sufficient for IoT tasks and wins on price and power use. The Pi Zero only has a single USB connector and no networking. The Pi Zero W, more expensive at $15, has onboard WiFi and if you want a connected device it is the obvious choice.

Both the Pi Zero and the Pi Zero W have a single-core CPU, which means your program will be interrupted by the operating system to keep the device working. In many applications this doesn't matter, but if it does then the latest in the family, the Pi Zero 2W has a quad-core CPU, costs the same as the Pi Zero W and otherwise has the same specification. It is based on the same CPU as the Pi 3 and has a very similar overall architecture.

Pi Zero – small and low cost   Pi Zero W – with WiFi   Pi Zero 2W - four cores

Pi Zero	Pi Zero W	Pi Zero 2W
No WiFi	802.11 b/g/n wireless LAN	802.11 b/g/n wireless LAN
No Bluetooth	Bluetooth 4.1	Bluetooth 4.2
No Bluetooth	Bluetooth Low Energy (BLE)	Bluetooth Low Energy (BLE)
1GHz, single-core CPU	1GHz, single-core CPU	1GHz, quad-core CPU
512MB RAM	512MB RAM	512MB RAM
No Ethernet	No Ethernet	No Ethernet
Micro USB	Micro USB	Micro USB

Going Beyond The Pi Zeros

The original Raspberry Pis were available as an A or a B sub-type. The As lacked multiple USB connectors and a wired network connection and so were slightly cheaper. Since the Pi 4 there has only been the B version.

Another confusing factor is that when the Pi 3 was upgraded to have a quad-core processor, making it slightly faster, and doubling its memory, the two models were the Pi 3A+ and Pi 3B+.

These are the only members of the Pi 3 range still readily available and in terms of price only the 3A+, costing $25, has any advantage as the 3B+ at $35 costs the same as a Pi 4 B with the same amount (1GB) of memory.

Pi 3A+
802.11 b/g/n/ac wireless LAN 2.4 GHz and 5.0 GHz
Bluetooth 4.2
Bluetooth Low Energy (BLE)
1.4GHz, quad-core CPU 64-bit CPU
512MB RAM
One USB 2 port
No Ethernet

The Pi 3A

Until the arrival of the Pi 5, the Pi 4 was the fastest Pi available. The cheapest version with 1GB of RAM is the same price as a 3B+ ($35). At the top end of the range the 8GB version costs $75, which is starting to be expensive for IoT applications – even so you get a lot of computing power for the money. It also supports dual HDMI monitors, making it ideal for development purposes. You can also buy a P400 ($70) which is a Pi 4 with 4GB of RAM built into a keyboard, ready to use as a desktop computer.

Pi 4
802.11 b/g/n/ac wireless LAN 2.4 GHz and 5.0 GHz
Bluetooth 4.2
Bluetooth Low Energy (BLE)
1.8 GHz, quad-core 64-bit CPU
1, 2, 4 or 8 GB RAM
USB 2 and 3
Gigabit Ethernet

The Pi 4

The Pi 5 is currently the top of the range. Its specifications don't really tell the whole story. It has improved I/O connectivity, which speeds up the USB and Ethernet. It is roughly twice as fast as the Pi 4 and costs $60 with 4GB of RAM and $80 for 8GB. Although it represents excellent value, $60 per unit is starting to sound expensive for IoT deployments. It is still worth considering using one for software development, even if the application eventually ends up running on a less powerful device.

Pi 5
802.11 b/g/n/ac wireless LAN 2.4GHz and 5Ghz.
Bluetooth 5
Bluetooth Low Energy (BLE)
2.4GHz, quad-core CPU
4 or 8GB RAM
Gigabit Ethernet
USB 3

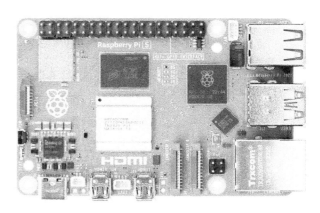

The Pi 5

The use of a custom interface chip, the RP1, makes the Pi 5 incompatible with all previous Pis from the point of view of peripherals including the GPIO lines. If you use GPIO Zero then any differences are hidden by the use of Linux drivers which iron out the differences between the Pi 5 and the rest of the range.

At the time of writing there is no indication of when a P500 self-contained computer version is likely to launch.

The Compute Module 4, CM4, is a cut down Pi 4. All of the external connectors have been removed and signals are only available on a high density connector on the bottom of the board. This is a full Pi 4 and the software you write for a main Pi model needs little, if any, change to run on it, but you will need to design a PCB motherboard for it to use to connect to the outside world. At the moment there is no CM5, but one is in the works and should be available sometime in 2024.

The Compute Module is only necessary if you are planning to develop hardware to complement the Pi as well as custom software.

The CM4

The Raspberry Pi Pico

Despite its name, the Pico isn't in the same family as either the Pi Zeros or the Pi 3/4/5s. It is a small device about the same size as the Pi Zero, but it is very different in that it uses a custom, two-core, CPU and doesn't run Linux. If you plan to create an IoT program that doesn't need Linux, then you are probably much better off moving to the Pico. It is low-cost and powerful and the fact that it doesn't host an operating system often makes developing code easier than trying to fit in with the way an operating system works. On the other hand, if you want local user interaction by way of a display, keyboard, touch screen, mouse, etc, then the Pico might not be the right choice.

In short, the Pico is a microcontroller capable of sensing and control tasks and communicating via the network, whereas those in the Pi family are full computers running Linux capable of sensing and control tasks. The book to get you started with the Pico is *Programming The Raspberry Pi Pico/W in MicroPython, 2nd Ed*, ISBN:9781871962796,

The Pico W

Pi OS

One additional complication is the choice of operating system for the Pi. The latest Pi OS is based on Debian Bookworm and is available in 32- and 64-bit versions for the Pi 4 and 5. For all the other Pis, currently the only OS available is the "legacy" Debian Bullseye. It is possible that Bookworm will become available on these "smaller" Pis in the future, but the main differences between the two aren't important. A bigger difference affects any program planning to make use of graphics. Bookworm has taken the big step of using Wayland in place of the X graphics system that Bullseye uses. In most cases you can isolate your programs from this change by using a suitable graphics library, but if you plan to interact at a low level with graphics you need to find out more about Wayland.

As far as GPIO Zero goes there is no essential differences between the two operating system versions.

What To Expect

There are no complete projects in this book – although some examples come very close and it is clear that some of them could be used together to create finished projects. The focus here is on learning how things work so that you can move on and do things that are non-standard. What matters is that you can reason about what the processor is doing and how it interacts with the real world in real time. This is the key difference between desktop and embedded programming: timing matters in embedded programming, but not so much in desktop programming.

This is a book about understanding the general principle and making things work. If you read to the end of this book you will have a good understanding of what is going on when you make use of a range of different types of interfacing that typically go together to make a complete system.

What Do You Need?

To follow the examples in this book you will need either a Pi Zero/W/2W or a Pi 3/4/5. You can use an earlier Pi as long as you make allowances for the difference in pin assignments and other minor hardware changes.

It is also worth knowing that while the Pi 4 and Pi 5 are capable of running a development environment and running IoT programs, the Pi Zero makes things hard work. If you want the simplicity of local development, discussed in Chapter 2, use a Pi 4 or 5.

Whichever model of Pi you use, you need it set up with Pi OS, the new name for Raspbian, and you need to know how to connect to it and use it via a serial console. You also need to be comfortable with Linux in the sense that while you might not know how to do something, you know how to look it up and follow the instructions. It is also assumed that you can program in Python. The level of Python required to understand the programs isn't high but you should be familiar with using modules and functions.

As to additional hardware over and above the Pi you will need a solderless prototype board and some hookup wires – known as Dupoint wires. You will also need some LEDs, a selection of resistors, some 2N2222 or other general purpose transistors and any of the sensors used in later chapters. It is probably better to buy what you need as you choose to implement one of the projects, but an alternative is to buy one of the many "getting started" kits for the Raspberry Pi. You will probably still need to buy some extra components, however.

A solderless prototype board and some Dupoint wires

You don't need to know how to solder, but you will need to be able to hook up a circuit on a prototyping board. A multimeter (less than $10) is useful, but if you are serious about building IoT devices investing in a logic analyzer (less than $50) will repay itself in no time at all. You can get small analyzers that plug in via a USB port and use an application to show you what is happening. It is only with a multichannel logic analyzer can you have any hope of understanding what is happening. Without one and the slight skill involved in using it, you are essentially flying blind and left to just guess what might be wrong.

A Low Cost Logic Analyzer

Finally, if you are even more serious, then a low-cost pocket oscilloscope is also worth investing in to check out the analog nature of the supposedly digital signals that microcontrollers put out. However, if you have to choose between these two instruments the logic analyzer should be your first acquisition.

It is worth noting that the Pi can generate signals that are too fast to be reliably detected by low-cost oscilloscopes and logic analyzers which work at between 1MHz and 25MHz. This can mean that working with pulses much faster than 1 microsecond can be difficult as you cannot rely on your instruments.

Safety In Numbers

A final point to make about the Raspberry Pi and its ecosystem regards the size of its user base. According to the Raspberry Pi Foundation, by August 2023 the Pi had sold more than 50 million units and while these aren't all exactly the same device they are all compatible enough to ensure that your programs have a good chance of running on any of them.

The large numbers of Pis in the world means that you have a good chance of finding the answer to any problem by a simple internet search, although it has to be said that the quality of answers available vary from misleading to excellent. Always make sure you evaluate what you are being advised in the light of what you know. You also need to keep in mind that the advice is also usually offered from a reasonably biased point of view. The C programmer will give you an answer that suits a system that already uses C, and electronics beginners will offer you solutions that are based on "off the shelf" modules when a simple cheap solution is available based on a few cheap components. Even when the advice you get is 100% correct, it still isn't necessarily the right advice for you.

The large numbers of Raspberry Pis in circulation also means that it is unlikely that the device will become obsolete. This isn't something you can assume about other less popular single-board computers. It is reasonable to suppose that any programs you write today will work into the foreseeable future on a device that might not look like today's Raspberry Pis but will be backward compatible.

In short, the Raspberry Pi provides a secure and non-threatening environment for your development work.

The Book's Roadmap

After covering how to get started with Python on the Pi using Thonny we take a look at the basic ideas of using Python to work with the GPIO lines and then take a detour into object-oriented Python – just enough to understand what GPIO Zero is doing.

From here we look in detail at simple on/off devices and show how to create custom devices. Although devices are what you most often use, the lowest-level approach is to use the Pin class and gain direct access to a GPIO line via a pin factory. The next chapter goes over the sort of basic electronics you need to get started with the IoT – it's not all you will ever need', but we hope it is enough to stop you destroying your Pi and whatever you connect to it.

From here we move on to simple, complex and internal input devices. This is also an introduction to GPIO Zero's ingenious source/values approach to declarative programming. We not only look at the basics, but show how to create custom classes to work with source/values.

Chapter 10 marks a shift in topic away from simple devices and GPIO lines to look at higher-level protocols – pulse width modulation, PWM, in this case. PWM is used for all sorts of things PWM it is commonly used with servo and DC motors and the next chapter deals with motors of all kinds, including unidirectional and bidirectional motors, with the help of an H bridge, servos, brushless DC motors and stepper motors, including a custom stepper motor device.

GPIO Zero has a feature whereby you can group different devices into larger compound devices. In Chapter 12 we explain the basics of the supplied devices and show how to use the idea to improve on the custom stepper motor device introduced earlier.

The next two chapters are all about the SPI bus. Starting from the basics and the supported SPI devices, we move on to consider how the SPI bus works and implement a custom SPI device.

The final chapter is about lgpio which is the library used to implement GPIO Zero on all versions of the Pi including the Pi 5.

Summary

- The cost of computing hardware has fallen to the point where many applications that would have used low-cost and less-powerful microcontrollers can now make use of Raspberry Pi hardware, which is powerful enough to run a full version of Linux.

- The smallest member of the Pi family is the Pi Zero. It has a single-core processor with a minimal number of connectors. The Pi Zero W has built-in WiFi which makes it easy to use in situations where you want connectivity. As well as WiFi, the Pi Zero 2W has four cores.

- The Pi 5 is currently the most powerful of the Pi models. Like the Pi 4, it is a quad-core device with up to 8Gb of RAM, but it is at least twice the speed of the Pi 4.

- As neither the Pi 5 or 4 isn't currently available as a "cut down" model A, the Pi 3A+ is still a viable choice for IoT applications.

- The Compute Module 4 (CM4) is a Pi 4 packaged as a credit card sized industrial device. It needs a custom I/O board or a development board to make use of it. The corresponding CM 5 should be available sometime in 2024.

- The Pi 400 is a faster Pi 4 with 4GB of RAM packaged into a keyboard. You can use it as an IoT development system. Currently there is no indication if and when a Pi 500 will be available.

- To work with electronics you will need a solderless prototyping board, some hookup wires and some components. It's also good to have a multimeter and preferably a logic analyzer. After these basic instruments, you can add what you can afford.

- With more than 50 million devices sold and a very large community of users, the Raspberry Pi is a very stable platform and one you can use with reasonable assurance that it will be available in the future.

Chapter 2

Getting Started With Python And GPIO Zero

The most difficult part of any project is getting started. Once you have managed it, you can't see what the difficulty was in the first place! In this case it is assumed that you have your Pi up and running and can work with it either via a screen, keyboard and mouse, a Secure Shell (SSH) connection or using remote desktop.

You can work with Python using a range of different approaches and they each have their advantages and disadvantages. In the first instance it is probably best to choose the easiest option and in the case of the Pi that is to use Thonny as it is already installed and ready to go, as is Python 3. You can use this setup on any Pi and use them to develop and run programs, but the Pi Zero struggles to keep up.

A better solution is to use remote development. That is to use another machine to create and edit the program and run it on a target machine that is connected via SSH. Thonny supports remote development but at the time of writing it doesn't support remote debugging. This makes it less than perfect but it is the simplest way to get started with remote development.

If you move on to be more ambitious you might want to develop Python programs using Visual Studio Code (VS Code) running on a desktop Windows, Mac or Linux machine. VS Code supports full remote debugging and an extensive range of tools to make programming easier. How to get started with VS Code is described in Appendix I but, while not difficult, it takes many steps to get it all working and you might want to leave it until you need it.

Your First Python Pi Program

It is assumed that you have your Pi set up and you can work with a desktop, either locally or remotely. In most cases the simplest way to get started is to add a keyboard, mouse and monitor to a Pi 4 or 5. In this case you are using local development i.e. the same machine is being used to develop and test the program.

An alternative is to use a remote desktop connection VNC or RDP to a Pi that doesn't have a monitor, keyboard and mouse – a so called headless Pi.

If you do want to work with a headless Pi then an even easier solution is to use remote development via another Pi or a desktop machine – see the next section.

If you do opt for local development and it is by far the easiest way to get started, then you will find that Python, GPIO Zero and the Thonny code editor are already installed and ready to use.

Drop down the main menu and in the Programming sub-menu select Thonny. The IDE will open for you:

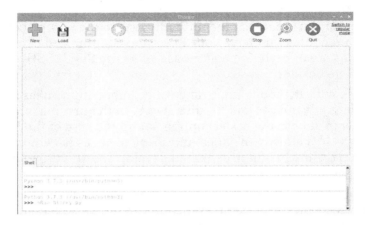

You can start to program at once. Click the New icon and enter the single line program:

```
print("Hello Python World")
```

If you now click the Run icon you will be prompted to save the file, create a new directory if you want to and save the file as "hello". Once you have done this your program will run and you will see:

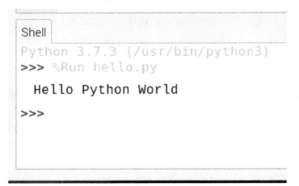

Yes, it really is this easy to get started with Python programming on a Raspberry Pi, but in many cases you will need to do a little more.

Remote Development

If you are using Thonny on a powerful enough Pi then developing GPIO Zero programs on the machine that is running them works well enough. If you are using a Pi Zero then things are not so good. The Pi Zero is only just fast enough to cope with running Thonny and if you try to test an IoT program on the same machine you will find that the demands made on a single-core processor are too great for many situations. The same is true to a lesser extent of the Pi Zero 2W which doesn't really have enough memory to run Thonny and other programs at the same time. Local development is really only good on a Pi 4 or Pi 5. Another problem with local development is that you generally want to develop an IoT program on one machine and then move it to another to try out different configurations. Local development stores the program on a single machine and moving it to another machine and running it is often a burden.

A solution to this problem is to use a remote development approach. That is, run Thonny on one machine and run the Python programs you create on another. As Python is an interpreted language, and hence needs no compile stage, this is particulary easy to do. You can connect to the remote machine by SSH, transfer the file from the machine running Thonny to the remote machine and then run it. Of course, this supposes that you have an SSH connection set up. In most cases what you need is a headless Pi with a predefined SSH connection. This is most easy to do when you create an SD card with the OS using the Raspberry Pi Imager. You can set up the details of the WiFi in the General Tab of the OS Customization:

You can setup the SSH connection on the next tab:

In many cases you need to use public-key authentication to avoid having to type in the password each time you make a connection to the machine. Thonny copes well, however, with using a password so Use password authentication is a reasonable choice. Notice that this means that only the single user setup on the first page can connect via SSH, but you can set up other users once the machine has booted.

Once you have created the SD card, you can boot the Pi without needing a keyboard, mouse or monitor. If you want to work with it directly then you need an SSH client such as Putty. This lets you connect to the headless machine and use the command line. In most cases however you don't need to do this as Thonny will make the SSH connection to the headless Pi for you. To make use of this, Thonny has to be in "regular" mode which is also the recommended way to use it.

Once in regular mode all you need to do is select Run and then select the Interpreter tab from the dialog and enter the details of the remote machine and the account to use:

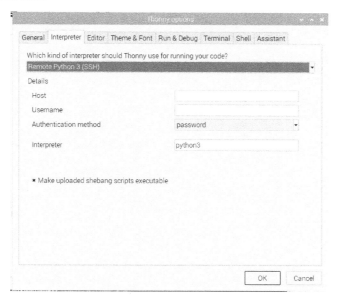

You can often use the Host name that you set in the Raspberry Pi Imager in the Host field. If this fails you need to use the headless Pi's IP address, which can be difficult to find without help. There are IP address scanners that can be used to find the IP address. For example: Advanced IP Scanner at `https://www.advanced-ip-scanner.com/`.

As already discussed, the simplest way to get started is to use a username and password to connect via SSH. You need to make sure that you can connect to the Pi using the specified credentials.

If everything is specified correctly you should be able to run your program on the headless Pi by simply selecting Run. The program will automatically be downloaded to the Pi and run remotely.

So, if you enter:

```
from gpiozero import Device
Device()
print(Device.pin_factory.board_info.model)
```

You can run this automatically on the headless Pi and you will see the model type displayed in the shell at the bottom of the screen:

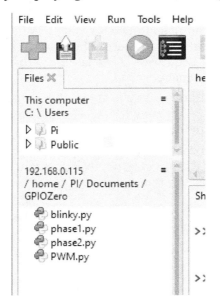

You can see and manage the state of the files stored on the local and the remote machine by displaying the File window using View, Files

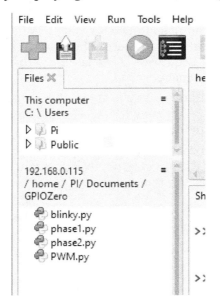

You can right-click on any file or folder on either machine and transfer them to the other machine.

Finally, you can use Thonny to open a shell to the remote machine and to submit commands. To open a shell use Tools.Open system shell. You have to supply the users password.

Thonny is easy to get started with and to use, but it lacks a good remote debugger and other features that more sophisticated code editors have. Even so for many beginners Thonny is the best first choice and you can go a long way using nothing more.

Summary

- The easiest way to create Python programs on a Pi is to run Thonny or one of the other IDEs on the Pi itself. This works reasonably well on the Pi 3/4/5, but not so well on the Pi Zero.

- Thonny can also be used for remote development using a headless Pi, i.e. one that doesn't have a keyboard, mouse or monitor connected.

- Connection to the headless Pi is via SSH. The simplest way of setting up a headless machine with SSH is to use the Raspberry Pi Imager and specify a WiFi to connect to, a user and to enable SSH.

- To connect to the remote machine you simply select the Python interpreter to use to run the program.

- Thonny allows you to manage files on both the local and remote machines. It also allows you to open a shell to the remote machine that you can use to give commands.

- At the time of writing, Thonny does not support remote debugging. If you want more sophisticated support including remote debugging you need to move to VS Code, see Appendix I.

Chapter 3

Introduction to the GPIO

GPIO Zero is a sophisticated way to work with devices connected to a Pi, but it is all built on some very basic features provided by the GPIO (General Purpose IO) lines. It is important to understand how all of this works and in particular how it works with GPIO Zero, so in this chapter we look at how to get started with the IoT in Python by writing what most people consider to be the "Hello World" of IoT or "Blinky". All this does is to flash an LED at a steady rate – hence "Blinky". It may be simple, but it serves the purpose of getting you to know how to control a GPIO line and is a good starting point.

GPIO?

The term GPIO is used a lot and usually without bothering to define what it means. It stands for General Purpose Input Output and it is the fundamental way a device like the Pi connects to the outside world. A GPIO line is a pin that can be used to connect to another device via a wire. The line can be configured to be an input or an output and software can read and write its current state. Some programs make use of the GPIO lines raw in that they read and write data directly from and to the lines. Other types of output that you will meet later use GPIO lines to implement more specialized forms of communication and in this case the software doesn't directly make use of the GPIO lines involved but asks the more sophisticated hardware to do the job.

GPIO Zero, despite its name, is all about moving away from the use of raw GPIO lines. It is about increasing the level of abstraction that we are working with. For example, you can take a single GPIO line and connect it to an LED and you can set the LED on and off by controlling the GPIO line in software. This works but an arguably better method is to implement in software an LED object which can be programmed in terms like LED.on and LED.off rather than having to consider the details of using the GPIO line. Of course a GPIO line is involved in the process even if its use is hidden by the software – when you state LED.on a GPIO line is set high and the LED connected to it lights up.

GPIO Zero provides classes to let you work with a range of objects from traffic lights to motors and robots. However they all use GPIO lines to do their work.

31

A First IoT Program

The purpose of this program is to just let you check that everything is working, the functions used will be explained in detail later.

Start a new program called `blinky`. Then enter the program:

```
from gpiozero import LED
from time import sleep

led = LED(4)

while True:
        led.on()
        sleep(1)
        led.off()
        sleep(1)
```

You don't have to install `gpiozero` or `sleep` as they are standard modules on a Pi. Even though you don't know much about GPIO Zero just yet, it isn't difficult to understand what is going on in the program. First we create an LED Python object associated with GPIO4 and then an infinite loop turns the LED on and off with a pause of 1 second between each action. The LED on command sets GPIO4 to a high voltage and the off command sets it low – on/off or high/low its the same thing.

If this works, GPIO4 which is Pin 7 on the Pi's connector, is set to be an output and then the loop turns it on and off (high voltage then low) with a delay of one second.

The library uses logical GPIO numbers assigned within the Pi's processor. These GPIO lines are brought out to the Pi's connector and the logical GPIO numbers don't correspond to the pins on the connector. In this case GPIO4 is Pin 7 on connector P1.

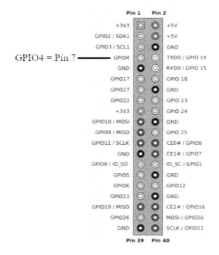

If you want to connect an LED to see the "blinking" for real then this is easy enough, but you do need a current-limiting resistor - 200Ω is a good choice. The reason for the resistor is explained in Chapter 7.

How you build the circuit is up to you. You can use a prototyping board or just a pair of jumper wires. The short pin and/or the flat on the side of the case marks the negative connection on the LED - the one that goes to Pin 6.

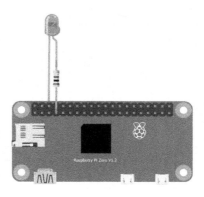

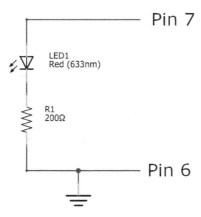

If you can't be bothered to go through the ritual of testing "blinky" with a real LED, then just connect a logic analyzer to Pin 7 and you will see 1-second pulses.

Pin Numbering

Something that drives every programmer mad is the different ways of referring to the numbering of the GPIO pins. There is the physical pin number, i.e. the number of the pin on the physical connector, and the logical GPIO number, which is assigned deep in the hardware.

For most of the Pi family the standard 40-pin connector is largely the same:

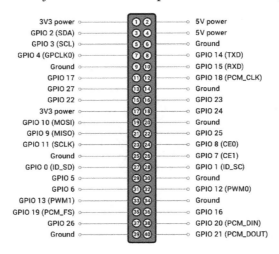

GPIO Zero works in terms of logical pin numbers so you need to use these diagrams to look up which physical pin you have to connect to. So for example, "GPIO4", or just 4, specifies physical pin 7. You can also use the notation "header:pin" where header is the name of the connector. So for example, "J8:7" is Pin 7, i.e. GPIO4 on modern Pis. Another alternative is to use the notation "BOARDpin" e.g. "BOARD7" is Pin 7, i.e. GPIO4. It doesn't matter how you specify the pin to use, it is automatically converted to the GPIO pin number and this is how the pin number is returned if you request it.

If you study the diagrams, you will see that there are many GPIO lines – GPIO1 to GPIO27. There are other GPIO lines. Some are used internally by the Pi to do things like control a status LED and some are simply not brought out to the connector. In some cases you can gain access to the lines that are used internally, but in most cases this isn't a good idea as making the physical connection is difficult.

The command `pinout` can be used from the console to see the pins and the general configuration of the device you are using:

```
J8:
    3V3  (1) (2)  5V
  GPIO2  (3) (4)  5V
  GPIO3  (5) (6)  GND
  GPIO4  (7) (8)  GPIO14
    GND  (9) (10) GPIO15
 GPIO17 (11) (12) GPIO18
 GPIO27 (13) (14) GND
 GPIO22 (15) (16) GPIO23
    3V3 (17) (18) GPIO24
 GPIO10 (19) (20) GND
  GPIO9 (21) (22) GPIO25
 GPIO11 (23) (24) GPIO8
    GND (25) (26) GPIO7
  GPIO0 (27) (28) GPIO1
  GPIO5 (29) (30) GND
  GPIO6 (31) (32) GPIO12
 GPIO13 (33) (34) GND
 GPIO19 (35) (36) GPIO16
 GPIO26 (37) (38) GPIO20
    GND (39) (40) GPIO21
```

Finding a pin can be difficult without a printed label and there are a number of aids on the market:

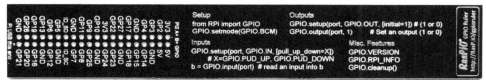

RasPiO® GPIO Ruler from Pimoroni

The most common way of doing the job without a label is to count from the top or the bottom of the inner or outer column of pins. The following diagram makes this slightly easier:

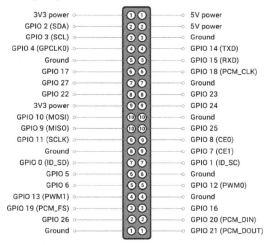

Notice that the pin number is supposed to start from one at each end of the connector – its is what makes the counting easier!

GPIO Modes

Although GPIO Zero gives you access to devices like LEDs, which means you can mostly ignore the basic GPIO lines, you still have to select which one to use and this isn't quite as easy as it looks.

The available GPIO lines are shown in the following diagram:

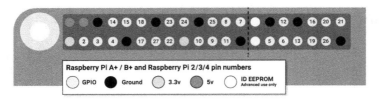

You may also notice that many of the pins on the pinout diagrams have two labels. For example, GPIO2 is also labeled as SDA1. Many, but not all, of the GPIO lines have alternative functions such as connecting SPI devices, more of which later. In general, you should avoid using pins which have an alternative function as general-purpose I/O lines. The reason is that you might need to use one of the special functions later in your project's development and, if it is is already used as a GPIO line, you will not only have to change all the pin assignments, which is relatively easy, but also all of the hardware connections, which is harder. This is much less of a problem if you restrict yourself to basic GPIO Zero as it supports many features via software that works on any pin. However, you may want to go outside GPIO Zero and use the alternative functions of the GPIO lines.

In practice, for general GPIO tasks use:

GPIO 4, 5, 6, 12, 13, 17, 18, 22, 23, 24, 25, 26 and 27

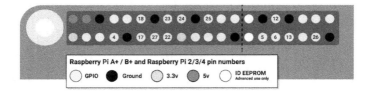

The "preferred" GPIO pins.

Then use:

GPIO 2, 3, 9, 7, 8, 16, 10, 11, 14, 15, 19, 20 and 21

in that order. The reason for the non-sequential order is that some GPIO lines work as a group and once you have used one you might as well use the others.

This isn't a definitive rule because the Pi 4/5 offers additional modes for many of the GPIO lines. Although the situation is very complicated, don't worry too much as changing which GPIO line is being used in software is easy and, unless you have reached a late prototyping stage, it is fairly easy in hardware.

Hardware and Software Working Together

Although Blinky is a very simple program it is typical of the process of working with IoT projects and some of the comments made at the start of the chapter should make more sense. All IoT projects are a combination of hardware and software. Usually you have to connect some device to a set of GPIO lines. In some cases you can select which lines you want to use, but in others the lines are fixed and you have to use the lines that are specified.

Once you are happy that the device is connected to the GPIO lines and powered properly, you can move on to the software. In most cases you will be able to use a GPIO Zero class designed to work with the device. Then all you have to do is specify the GPIO pins you have used to connect the device, if they aren't fixed, and then use the methods provided to control the device. In many cases the device can be so abstracted from GPIO lines that you can forget that they exist. Even the humble LED works in terms of On and Off with no reference to the GPIO line being set "high" or "low". More complicated devices hide the fact that they are working with particular GPIO lines almost completely and even the notion of on and off or high and low vanishes. However, you need to keep in mind that the inputs and outputs of the Pi really are just GPIO lines that change state from high to low and low to high.

In later chapters we look not only at the standard devices that GPIO Zero supports, but how to create classes that make new devices easier to work with.

Summary

- A first IoT program is particularly easy in GPIO Zero. The standard Blinky example only needs an LED object and the use of its on and off methods. All you have to do is assign a GPIO line and connect an LED to it.

- Pin numbering is complicated by the fact that there are GPIO numbers and physical pin numbers. The simplest thing to do is to always use the GPIO numbers as assigned by the processor and convert these to pin numbers when you connect up.

- The `pinout` command used at the Pi console will print a map of the pins.

- You can buy labels that help find a particular pin or just adopt the technique of counting pins from either end on the inside or outside row of the connector.

- Not all of the GPIO lines that the Pi has are brought out on the main connector. Some are used internally and some are simply ignored.

- Some of the GPIO lines have alternative functions and these are best avoided if all you need is a simple GPIO input/output line.

- All IoT projects are a mix of hardware and software. Usually there is a phase where you experimentally connect the hardware and write some instructions just to check that you have it connected correctly before moving on to creating the real project.

Chapter 4

Python - Class and Object

Although this is not a book designed to teach you Python, before we go any further we are making a detour into some specific aspects of the language. This is because your first encounter with GPIO Zero might have confused you if you don't know about classes and objects. Many Python programmers are hardly aware that Python is object-oriented. The reason is that Python is designed to be easy to get started with and this means that you can immediately start to write a program simply as a few lines of code. Later you might learn about functions and organize your code in a better way, but there is no real pressure on you to learn about classes and objects which are arguably an even better way to organize your code.

This account is a very pragmatic look at the way Python implements objects and it is certainly not complete or extensive. If you really want to understand what is going on and why it all fits together in a remarkably elegant way you need to read Programmer's Python: Everything Is An Object, 2nd Ed , ISBN:978-1871962741 in which Mike James looks at the deeper logic of the Python's approach to objects.

GPIO Zero is an object-oriented library and as such you cannot avoid using classes and objects. When you write:

```
from gpiozero import LED
led = LED(4)
while True:
    led.on()
    led.off()
```

you are using classes, objects and methods. LED is a class that you use to create an object, an instance of the LED class. A reference to the new object is stored in the variable led and you use this to access the object. Notice that led is not the object, but a reference to the object.

There can be more than one reference to an object. For example:

```
led1 = LED(4)
led2=led
```

Now both led1 and led2 reference the same object. You can think of led2 and led as "pointing" at the same object which lives somewhere else in memory. This is a subtle, but important, idea.

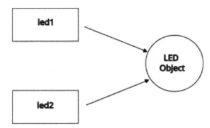

When you use led.on() you are using one of the methods of the LED class that the instance supports.

All of this is fairly easy and you can simply make use of it at an intuitive level. You can create new programs by simply following the lead that GPIO Zero sets and accepting that this is just "the way things are done". A much better idea, however, is to use it as an opportunity to learn about Object-Oriented Python. Even if you know the basics, there are many advanced techniques used in GPIO Zero and understanding them will improve your Python programs.

If you know all about objects in Python skim read this chapter to make sure you haven't forgotten or missed anything. You are expected to already know the basics of Python, such as control statements, if, the while and for loops and functions.

Objects

The idea of an object is relatively old in programming, but it has taken time for it to become mainstream.

When we first started writing programs in higher-level languages, best practice was to write a function for whatever you needed to do.

For example, if you needed to sort an array, you would write a sort function which accepted a few parameters that determined the data and the operation:

```
sort(myArray,order)
```

where myArray is the data that you want to sort, and order is a parameter that sets the sort order to be used.

Later on we moved over to object-oriented programming where data and the functions that process the data are grouped together into entities called objects. In this case functions such as sort became methods of the data that they were to operate on.

So an Array object would have a sort method and you would write the sort operation as:

```
myArray.sort(order)
```

You can see that this is a small change from the use of `myArray` as a parameter to the sort function to using `myArray` as an object with a sort method. You could say that the shift from functions to object-oriented programming is all about the shift of a parameter from inside the function to outside it.

Looking a little deeper, the simplification that this shift brings about is well worth it. The sort function can now use the data in `myArray` more or less by default and this makes it possible to create an isolation from the rest of the program. It also brings about a complete change in the way that we think about functions.

For example, you could say that `myArray` "knows how" to sort itself. Another object, `myList` say, may also "know how" to sort itself using its own sort function, which isn't the same as the `Array` sort function. This is usually referred to as polymorphism – the same function `sort` changes its form depending on the object it belongs to.

So instead of having to write:

```
if A==Array:
        ArraySort(A)
else:
        ListSort(A)
```

we can just write:

```
A.sort()
```

It also means that we think about creating not just an `array`, which is a collection of data, but an `Array` object which is data and code.

In the case of GPIO Zero there is an even more appropriate interpretation. For example:

```
led.on()
```

can be thought of as the LED object "knowing how" to turn itself on. The alternative is to have an on function which "knows how" to turn any LED on:

```
on(led)
```

You can see that thinking of an LED as something that has built-in actions is a reasonable and convenient approach.

41

Although we have been talking about actions, objects have attributes that are any type of data. For example:

```
print(led.value)
```

In this case the attribute value is 1 if the LED is on and 0 otherwise. Setting the attribute also changes the state of the LED, i.e. to turn it on you would use:

```
led.value=1
```

You can think of this as storage that is local to the instance. That is, if you create another LED:

```
led2=LED(5)
```

then it has its own value attribute.

Methods are just attributes that happen to be functions.

Creating Your Own Objects - Class

Using objects is easy, but there comes a time when you need to create your own objects. Creating a custom object is relatively easy, but it can seem involved when you first encounter it.

First you have to create a class which gives the definition of the object you want to create and then you use it to create as many instances of the class as you need. You already know how this works with objects that GPIO Zero provides. The LED class defines all of the attributes of any led objects you use it to create.

```
led=LED(4)
```

This use of class and instance is a slight problem when it comes to naming things. For example, the LED class has the name you might want to use for a single instance of the class. This is particularly irritating when all you want is a single instance of the class. Then, there is even a tendency to think, "Why do I need a class at all? Why can't I just create an object directly?" The answer is you can, but the class/instance approach is much more common. In general, use upper case names for classes and lower case for instances.

To create a custom object you first have to create a custom class using the class keyword:

```
class MyClass:
    def myMethod(self):
        print("myMethod called")
```

This creates MyClass with a single method myMethod which simply prints something. Once defined, you can use MyClass in the standard way:

```
myObject=MyClass()
myObject.myMethod()
```

which prints myMethod called.

42

The only possibly confusing part is the use of `self` in the method definition. If you refer back to the way a function is converted into a method then it should make sense. In Python when you define a method you use `self` as the first parameter. When you call the method, Python automatically sets `self` to the name of the instance. That is:

```
myObject.myMethod()
```

is converted into:

```
myMethod(myObject)
```

and hence `self` is set to `myObject`. This is the fundamental way that functions become methods and is exactly how Python does it. It is worth noting that the use of `self` is a convention and not enforced by the system. You could use `this` in JavaScript/C++/Java-style, but your programs would be less readable by another Python programmer.

We now have a basic way of adding method attributes to an object, but how do we add data attributes? The key thing is that each instance of a class has to have its own copy of the data attributes. The simplest way to do this is to make use of the "magic" __init__ method. It is one of Python's many "magic" methods which are used automatically by the system to do fixed things. In this case the system automatically calls __init__ whenever you use a class to create an object. That is when you write:

```
 myObject=MyClass()
```

then any __init__ method you may have defined in `MyClass` is called before the object instance is complete.

Now consider what happens if you write:

```
class MyClass:
    def __init__(self):
        self.myAttribute1=0
```

and then create an instance:

```
myObject=MyClass()
```

Now your custom __init__ is called and it creates a new attribute `self.myAttribute`. What do you think `self` is set to? As in the case of calling a method, `self` is set to the object being created, i.e. `myObject` in this case. The call to __init__ is equivalent to:

```
__init(myObject)
```

and the attribute creation is the same as:

```
myObject.myAttribute1=0
```

Just as whenever you assign to a variable it is created if it doesn't already exist, so when you assign to an attribute it is created if it doesn't already exist. Using this mechanism __init__ can create new attributes on the instance of the class that it is just creating.

All of this comes down to two practices when you create a new class:

◆ Create any data attributes within the __init__ function using self to reference the object being created, e.g. self.attribute = 0

◆ Create any methods in the body of the class using self as the first parameter, e.g. def method(self):

As an example we can implement a class that represents a 2-D co-ordinate:

```
class Point:
    def __init__(self,x,y):
        self.x=x
        self.y=y

    def sum(self):
        print(self.x+self.y)

    def distance(self):
        return self.x**2+self.y**2
```

Notice that in the __init__ function we create two attributes, x and y and store the values of the x and y parameters in them. This is how you can initialize attributes with values provided when the object is created. That is:

```
point=Point(1,2)
print(point.x)
```

displays 1. The methods are simple, but notice the use of self to refer to attributes of the current instance. That is, in the sum method self.x becomes point.x when the function is called. That is:

```
point.sum()
print(point.distance())
```

prints 3 and 5 respectively. Notice that distance returns a value but sum doesn't – both are valid methods. If you want to call another method from within a method, you have to use self in the same way as for data attributes, e.g. self.sum().

Inheritance

Very often you find that the new class you want is very much like an existing class. The obvious solution is to copy and paste the text of the old class as a starter for the new class. This is workable and it is how most code was "reused" in the past, but today we have other ways of doing the same job. Inheritance is how object-oriented languages like Python implement reuse.

If you write:

```
class myNewClass(myOldClass)
```

then myNewClass

 has all of the attributes of myOldClass just as if you had used copy and paste. Unlike copy and paste, however, the connection between the old and new is live. If you make a change to the old class, the change is also made to the new class – they share the same base code. The new class is said to "inherit from", "derive from" or "sub-class" the old class, which is its "base class" or "super class". This sounds useful because if you find an error in the base class you can correct it and the correction will be inherited by all of the derived classes. This is generally good but also dangerous. If the derived classes make any assumptions about the base class, then changes could result in all of them breaking. This is often called the problem of the "fragile" base class. Even so, many programmers agree that inheritance is better than copy and paste programming.

You can of course add attributes to the new class and you can provide replacements, or "override", methods that it inherits. For example, we can create a Point3D class from the Point class:

```
class Point3d(Point):
    def __init__(self,x,y,z):
        self.x=x
        self.y=y
        self.z=z
    def distance(self):
        return self.x**2+self.y**2+self.z**2
```

In this case we have inherited all of the methods of Point, but a new __init__ is used to create x,y and z as data attributes and we have overridden the inherited distance method to use the extra z attribute. Notice that you can still use the inherited sum method:

```
point=Point3d(1,2,3)
print(point.x)
point.sum()
print(point.distance())
```

which displays 1, 3 and 14.

Notice that you can modify and add to inherited attributes, but you cannot easily remove them. It is part of the object-oriented philosophy that classes get "bigger" as they are inherited – a Point3d object is "bigger" in the sense that it generally has more attributes than a Point object.

The Need For Super

The key idea is that a class inherits everything its super class has, but this isn't quite as simple as it sounds. Consider for a moment a small change to the Point3D class based on this idea. As the Point3D class inherits everything that the Point class has, we don't need to redefine the x and y attributes as these are inherited:

```
class Point3d(Point):
    def __init__(self,x,y,z):
        self.z=z
    def distance(self):
        return self.x**2+self.y**2+self.z**2
```

In this version we only define the new z attribute. If you try this out you will find that it generates an error reporting that one of x or y isn't defined.

The point is that Point3d doesn't inherit x and y from Point, but it does inherit its __init__ function which creates them. That is, to make Point3D inherit all of the attributes that Point has, it has to call Point.__init__():

```
class Point3d(Point):
    def __init__(self,x,y,z):
        Point.__init__(x,y)
        self.z=z
```

If you try this out you will find it doesn't work because the call to Point.__init__ doesn't have a value for self. In this case you have to explicitly pass a value for self that gives the instance being created.

So the correct version of calling the super class __init__ function is:

```
class Point3d(Point):
    def __init__(self,x,y,z):
        Point.__init__(self,x,y)
        self.z=z
```

This creates the x and y attributes as part of any instance that Point3d creates.

It is generally considered bad practice to call the methods belonging to the super using the name of the super class, i.e. Point in this example. It works for any super class method you want to call, but Python provides the super function to make this easier. The super function automatically returns the super class of the class it is called in and when you use it to call a super class method, it automatically supplies the self parameter.

So the best way to call the super class __init__ function is to use:

```
class Point3d(Point):
    def __init__(self,x,y,z):
        super().__init__(x,y)
        self.z=z
```

There are many variations on the use of super, but this is the most basic and the one you should know.

You have to remember that the idea that a class inherits everything from its super class is only true if you take the trouble to make it true. In general, you have to call the super class __init__ function and you have to make sure you pass the correct parameters to it to create the attributes you want.

Multiple Inheritance – The Mixin

So far we have regarded the idea of inheritance as a way of getting a starting point for a new class that is similar to an existing class. This idea is fundamental to the object-oriented philosophy, which goes well beyond simple practical concerns and considers that the inheritance of objects is key to the way we should program. You start out by creating very general classes and slowly use inheritance to derive increasingly more sophisticated and specific classes. This gives rise to an inheritance hierarchy. For example, GPIO Zero has a class hierarchy for output devices:

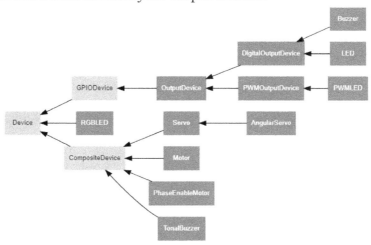

You can see that Device is at the top of the hierarchy and the classes become more specialized as you move down the hierarchy, i.e. move to the right in this rotated diagram. Thus Device is inherited by GPIODevice which is in turn inherited by OutputDevice, and then by DigitalOutputDevice and finally LED. This sort of hierarchy is supposed to be a model of the real world and the way we think about the relations between objects in the real world.

This works well when you are working with electronic devices that have obvious relationships, but don't let this fool you into thinking that this is the way object hierarchies work in the wider world. In the more general case, relationships between things are not well modeled by simple inheritance hierarchies and things are much more difficult. If you read up on object-oriented programming you will encounter many systems of rules, regulations and guidelines. If they make sense to you in the situation that you are programming in then by all means follow them, but the current state of programming theory is that no-one is in a position of authority to tell you how to program – it is all opinion.

If object-oriented programming theory is so problematic, why is it the most dominant method of programming? The simple answer is that even if, or perhaps especially if, you just regard it as a way of reusing code, then it is remarkably effective. Objects are a good way of packaging code that works together and providing it for others to use and inheritance is a good way to reuse code. It is also the case that objects are easy to use even if they are hard to invent and implement. In this sense we rely on other people to create a good set of objects for us to use and in this case the inheritance problem is their problem.

So, if a little inheritance is a good thing, why not multiple inheritance? That is, why not let a class inherit its attributes from multiple classes? This brings with it many problems, but the best known is the "diamond" problem – what happens if two base classes have an attribute of the same name? Which version of the attribute does the derived class use?

Because of this simple, but serious problem, many object-oriented languages, Java and C# for example, do not allow inheritance from more than one class. However, Python does. To solve the diamond problem, Python has a set of rules that determines which class attribute is used if there is a clash. If you want to know more look up the MRO (Method Order Resolution) algorithm in *Programmer's Python: Everything Is An Object, 2nd Ed*, ISBN:978-1871962741, but at this stage the best thing is to simply avoid inheriting from classes that have attributes with the same name. That is, if you keep things simple, multiple inheritance tends to just work.

To inherit from more than one class you simply have to write a list of base classes when you use the `class` statement. For example:

```
class myDerivedClass(Base1,Base2, Base3):
```

Following this `myDerivedClass` has all the attributes of `Base1`, `Base2` and `Base3`. If by any chance they do have an attribute of the same name, then in this simple situation the MRO algorithm reduces to simply taking the first definition reading left to right. So if all three classes had a `myAttribute` attribute, the one defined in `Base1` would be used.

Multiple inheritance can be very complicated, confusing and error-prone, but there is one situation in which it is much easier, the mixin. This is just a base class used in multiple inheritance and has nothing new to add to the Python language – it is the way you think about it that is different. The normal flow of inheritance is that the derived class is a more elaborate version of the base class. An `LED` is a `DigitalOutputDevice` with some extra attributes specific to the `LED` object. It is the "is a" relationship that motivates the inheritance.

A mixin isn't a base class in the same sense. It is just a bundle of methods that you want to give a class without implying anything about a theoretical relationship. For example, suppose you create a `Debug` class complete with some useful debugging functions such as `name()` to print the name of the object, `create()` time of creation, etc. You might want to add the `Debug` class to a class, not because it is a type of `Debug` class, but just because the behavior added by the `Debug` class is useful. For example:

```
class LED(DigitalOutputDevice,Debug):
```

creates an `LED` class that inherits from `DigitalOutputDevice` in the sense that it "is a" `DigitalOutputDevice` and inherits some useful methods from the `Debug` mixin. This is a philosophical distinction, but sometimes a useful one. Notice that if we add `Debug` to `DigitalOutputDevice` then all of the classes that derive from it, `LED` and `Buzzer` in this case, also inherit `Debug`. A mixin works from the point of view of inheritance in the same way as any other class - it's how you think of it that is different.

There is one way that mixins often differ, but again it's a convention. Mixins generally only have methods and not data attributes. One reason for this is that it means that a derived class doesn't have to call the mixin's __init__ method and so using it is simpler. However, this is a convention and if your mixin needs some data attributes there is no real reason to avoid them and GPIO Zero certainly doesn't.

GPIO Zero has a number of useful mixins, but they tend to be difficult to understand because they do sophisticated things. For example, the `HoldMixin` adds a set of methods and data attributes to implement a `when_held` event, for example to detect when a `Button` is held down. It can be added to any class that the concept of "holding" makes sense.

Virtual Base Classes

If you study GPIO Zero you might be surprised at how many base classes there are. It almost certainly wasn't designed like that from the start and the hierarchy was most probably constructed by "refactoring", that is looking at what the classes were doing and taking common code to form simpler base classes. At the top of the class hierarchy should be the simplest class with methods that all the derived classes need. Some languages have the concept of a virtual class, a class that simply defines the attributes that any class derived from it has to have. This often serves as the base class for a hierarchy as it doesn't even implement the methods it defines, leaving that to the next derived class.

Python doesn't have virtual classes, but that doesn't stop GPIO Zero from using something that looks like a virtual class. If you look at the entire GPIO Zero class hierarchy, you will see that Device is the top of the hierarchy:

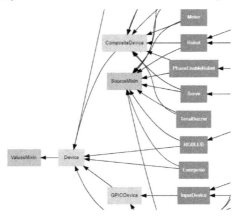

If you examine the code for Device you will find that, while it does have some methods and data attributes, one of its attributes is coded as:

```
@property
def value(self):
    """
    Returns a value representing the device's state. Frequently, this is a
    boolean value, or a number between 0 and 1 but some devices use larger
    ranges (e.g. -1 to +1) and composite devices usually use tuples to
    return the states of all their subordinate components.
    """

    raise NotImplementedError
```

You can see that this makes the class incomplete. It isn't intended to be used to create instances because part of the implementation is missing. Instead Device exists to be used as a base class for other devices - it is Python's equivalent of a virtual class.

Notice that a virtual class might well be used to create another virtual class that is more defined, but still too general to actually be used to create an instance. For example Device gives rise to GPIODevice which is slightly more specific, but perhaps not developed enough to be used to create an instance.

Attributes and Properties

A data attribute is the simplest way of allowing an object to store data. In this case you can simply use the attribute as if it was a variable. For example:

```
myObject.myAttribute = 42
```

Attributes work well but they are the first step on the way to more sophisticated approaches to storing data. For example suppose you have a data attribute that is used to store the temperature:

```
MyObject.temperature = 42
```

If this was being used to control the temperature of an enclosure via a heater it would be a good idea to check that it was set within a reasonable range, 20 to 30 °C say. It would also be useful if the temperature could be stored internally in millicentigrade, i.e. in thousandths of a centigrade degree, a unit often used by IoT devices. With a simple data attribute there is no way to do this, but you can easily invent one.

Instead of a data attribute we can create two methods, usually called get and set methods:

```
class Heater():
    def __init__(self):
        self.temperature=22*1000
    def setTemperature(self,t):
        if t<20:return
        if t>30:return
        self.temperature=t*1000
    def getTemperature(self):
        return self.temperature/1000
```

You can see that we now have a get and a set method and the set checks that the value is in range and the get converts back to centigrade. This all works, but it means you have to use the temperature attribute in an unnatural way:

```
heater=Heater()
heater.setTemperature(31)
print(heater.getTemperature())
```

Python has a better way. You can define a property using the @property decorator. Decorators are a powerful part of Python and if you want to know more see *Programmer's Python: Everything is an Object* but in this case we just want to make use of it.

For example:

```
class Heater():
    def __init__(self):
        self._temperature=22*1000
    @property
    def temperature(self):
        return self._temperature/1000
    @temperature.setter
    def temperature(self,t):
        print(t)
        if t<20:return
        if t>30:return
        self._temperature=t*1000
```

You can see that we have a get function and a set function defined in a slightly different way. We also need to have a "backing" variable, _temperature, because now we have named the getter and setter temperatures. This might seem slightly more complicated, but now you can write:

```
heater=Heater()
heater.temperature = 31
print(heater.temperature)
```

and the get and set functions are used automatically, i.e. the temperature doesn't change because it is outside of the range.

Properties are used for all sorts of reasons throughout GPIO Zero. For example, in Device you will find:

```
@property
def is_active(self):
    """
    Returns :data:`True` if the device is currently active and
    :data:`False` otherwise. This property is usually derived from
    :attr:`value`. Unlike :attr:`value`, this is *always* a boolean.
    """
    return bool(self.value)
```

This allows you to write things like:

```
if(device.is_active):
```

without having to convert to Boolean values or make a comparison.

Summary

- Python is an easy language to get started with, but this makes it possible to miss that it is an object-oriented language.

- After using Python for a while, beginners often have to go back and discover what makes Python object-oriented when they first encounter, and want to use and understand, an object-oriented library like GPIO Zero.

- Objects are packages of data and code that are related. The methods work on the data stored in the objects.

- Object-oriented code starts from the idea that you can convert `object.method()` into `method(object)`. The `self` parameter is used to perform this transformation in Python.

- An object is created as an instance of a class, which can be thought of as the specification for an object.

- To create your own classes you need the `class` keyword. You also need to use the __init__ magic method to create data attributes.

- One class, the derived class, can inherit all of the methods and attributes of another class, the base class. This allows for code reuse if a new class is essentially just an elaboration of an existing class.

- Derived classes have to ensure that that their base class instances are properly constructed and this usually involves calling the __init__ method of the base class using the `super` function.

- Python supports multiple inheritance where a derived class can inherit the properties and methods of multiple base classes. This can create problems if the base classes share attributes or methods with the same name.

- The mixin is a special, and simple, case of multiple inheritance where all that is required is to give a class a set of helper methods.

- Python doesn't have virtual classes, which simply act as definitions for the minimum set of properties a derived class has to have, but these can be easily simulated.

- Data attributes are simple, but often you need to perform some processing on a value when it is accessed. The best way to do this in Python is to use properties.

Chapter 5

Simple On/Off Devices

There are only two simple on/off devices – the LED and the Buzzer. In this chapter we look at each in turn and learn how to create our own new custom on/off devices.

On/Off Inheritance

The inheritance hierarchy for the simple output devices is:

If you don't know about inheritance then see the previous chapter.

Knowledge of the inheritance hierarchy is mostly useful in creating your own custom classes to extend GPIO Zero. Device is the most general and then we have GPIODevice which corresponds to a single GPIO line used as input or output. OutputDevice is a general output line, DigitalOutputDevice only has two states and finally LED and Buzzer correspond to real devices.

LED In Detail

The LED class is the archetypal on/off device. You have already seen how to create an LED object associated with a particular GPIO pin:

```
led = LED(4)
```

creates an LED object associated with GPIO4.

Other things you can specify when creating an LED object are:

```
LED(pin, active_high=True, initial_value=False, pin_factory=None)
```

Parameter	Action
active_high	If True the on method sets the line high If False the off method sets the line high
initial_value	If True the device is initially on If False the device is initially off
pin_factory	The underlying pin factory to use Let GPIO Zero set this

So for example:

```
led=LED(4, active_high=True, initial_value=True)
```

creates an LED associated with GPIO4 that is high when switched on and hence initially on.

There are only four methods associated with LED. The most commonly used are on and off which switch the LED on and off.

If you want to make the LED flash then you can use:

```
blink(on_time, off_time,n, background)
```

which will blink the LED *n* times, switching on for on_time and off for off_time specified in seconds. The background parameter defaults to True and this allows the blinking to be performed on another thread in the background. That is, if background is False, blink blocks and does not return until the *n* blinks have been completed, which brings your program to a halt. If you want to do other things while the LED is flashing then set background to True or accept the default. The LED will then flash *n* times after blink has returned.

For example, our original Blinky LED program given in Chapter 3:

```
from gpiozero import LED
from time import sleep
led = LED(4)
while True:
    led.on()
    sleep(1)
    led.off()
    sleep(1)
```

can be written as:

```
from gpiozero import LED
from signal import pause
led = LED(4)
led.blink(on_time=1,off_time=1,n=100)
print("Program Complete")
pause()
```

If you try this out you will discover that the LED keeps flashing for almost 200 seconds after the program has printed `Program Complete`. Notice that you need the pause at the end of the program because if your program comes to a halt so do any threads that the program has created. In short, without `pause()` you wouldn't see the LED flash at all. The point is that usually when you give a Python instruction you only move on to the next instruction when the current instruction has completed.

This is generally called "blocking" because the current instruction stops the next instruction executing before it is complete. The call to `blink` is non-blocking because it returns before it has finished everything you told it to do and the next instruction is executed while it is unfinished. Instructions that are non-blocking are very useful when working with hardware because it allows your program to get on with something else while the hardware is doing something.

Compare the behavior of the background non-blocking program with a blocking version:

```
from gpiozero import LED
led = LED(4)
led.blink(on_time=1,off_time=1,n=100,background=False)
print("Program Complete")
```

In this case you don't need the `pause()` because the program waits for the LED to have completed 100 flashes. You will only see the `Program Complete` message after 200 seconds.

It is interesting that in either case the `blink` method makes use of a new thread to run `LED` in the background, the only difference is that when `background` is `False` the main thread waits for the `blink` thread to complete.

The `toggle` method simply changes the LED from on to off or off to on depending on its current state. You can use it to write the Blinky program in yet another way:

```
from gpiozero import LED
from time import sleep

led = LED(4)

while True:
    led.toggle()
    sleep(1)
    led.toggle()
    sleep(1)
```

There are also some useful properties. The `is_lit` property is true if the LED is currently active and `value` sets and gets the state of the LED as a `1` or a `0`.

Finally we have the `pin` property which returns the pin object that the LED is connected to. The `Pin` object provides lower-level access to the GPIO line.

Buzzer

The only other standard on/off device is the buzzer and it goes on and off in the sense that it is driven by a single GPIO line, just like an LED, and makes a sound when the line is high and is silent when the line is low. It isn't capable of making different tones, it is either on or off.

The exact type of buzzer is a piezoelectric buzzer which emits a single tone and can be very loud:

You don't need a current-limiting resistor as buzzers take very little current. All you have to do is to make sure that it will operate at 3.3 volts. All you have to do to use one is connect the negative lead to ground and the positive lead to a GPIO line:

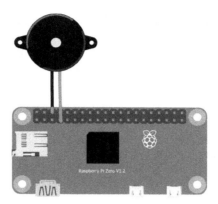

The Buzzer object has all of the properties and methods of the LED object. The on and off methods now make the buzzer sound but work in exactly the same way. The one small change is that blink is now renamed beep. It works in exactly the same way but now the buzzer is switched on and off.

```
from gpiozero import Buzzer
from signal import pause

buzz = Buzzer(4)
buzz.beep(on_time=1,off_time=1,n=100)
print("Program Complete")
pause()
```

You can see quite clearly that creating a Buzzer class is more about renaming things, so that your program can be more understandable, than introducing anything new.

A Custom On/Off Device

There are lots of on/off devices other than LED and Buzzer, so how do you arrange to work with them?

One solution is to treat everything as if it was an LED. For example, if you have an electric door lock you could write:

```
lock=LED(4)
lock.on()
...
lock.off()
```

It would work, but it might be confusing in the future when you have forgotten the program and are forced to wonder what an LED is doing with a lock and what lock.on() means.

A better and simpler solution is to derive a custom on/off device. You can do this using inheritance from `DigitalOutputDevice` which provides nearly all of the methods that `LED` has – in particular it has on and off methods. In this case we can simply pass the constructor parameters to the constructor of `DigitalOutputDevice`:

```
class Lock(DigitalOutputDevice):
    def __init__(self,*args,**kwargs):
        super().__init__(*args,**kwargs)
```

At this point `Lock` is really just a copy of `DigitalOutputDevice` and to customize it to be a `Lock` class we need to add appropriate methods. What we really need are two new methods, `lock` and `unlock`, and these can be implemented by calling the on and off methods of the super class:

```
def lock(self):
    super().on()
def unlock(self):
    super().off()
```

Now we have a `Lock` object that has `lock` and `unlock` methods that make sense for the device. However, we also still have on, off and blink which don't make any sense.

The simplest solution is to override them with methods that raise an appropriate exception:

```
def on(self):
  raise AttributeError("'Lock' object has no attribute 'on'")
def off(self):
  raise AttributeError("'Lock' object has no attribute 'off'")
def blink(self):
  raise AttributeError("'Lock' object has no attribute 'blink'")
```

This stops the use of the method calls, but the inappropriate attributes are still accessible. That is:

```
lock.on()
```

results in an exception, but:

```
myOn=lock.on
```

works, even if you can't actually call the method.

This is probably good enough for most use cases, but you could take it one step further by customizing the constructor. After all, you don't want to allow `active_high` to be set to `False` and have `lock` mean `unlock` and vice versa.

You can check for any keyword parameter using something like:

```
def __init__(self,*args,**kwargs):
    if 'active_high' in kwargs:
        raise TypeError("active_high not supported")
    super().__init__(*args,**kwargs)
```

If you would like a more specific error, you could define your own exception class.

You can carry on tailoring the behavior of Lock to be more lock-like until you have the perfect class. It is also a good idea to put your code into a module so that you can import Lock.

The complete program is:

```
from gpiozero import DigitalOutputDevice
class Lock(DigitalOutputDevice):
    def __init__(self,*args,**kwargs):
        if 'active_high' in kwargs:
            raise TypeError("active_high not supported")
        super().__init__(*args,**kwargs)
    def lock(self):
        super().on()
    def unlock(self):
        super().off()
    def on(self):
        raise AttributeError("'Lock' object has no attribute 'on'")
    def off(self):
        raise AttributeError("'Lock' object has no attribute 'off'")
    def blink(self):
        raise AttributeError("'Lock' object has no attribute 'blink'")
```

Using Lock is trivial:

```
office_door=Lock(4)

office_door.lock()
…
office_door.unlock()
```

You can use the same ideas to implement a custom class for any on/off device you care to use. What is interesting is that in practice customizing an existing class using inheritance is often as much about changing and restricting what the class can do as it is about extending it, which is not what textbooks emphasize most strongly.

This completes the software and it is worth remarking that simple locks of this sort are the same hardware problem as driving a solenoid. As these mostly work with 6 or 12 volts, you will need to use a transistor driver and you will need to take account of the voltage and the current involved, see the next chapter for more details.

Phased On/Off

There is a particular problem when you want to coordinate the times when devices switch on and off. Consider for a moment two LEDs that you want to flash in a phased way – led1 off when led2 is on and vice versa. You have to switch each LED as a separate operation and this means that there has to be a gap between the two actions. Consider for example the following program, which flashes two LEDs as fast as possible:

```
from gpiozero import LED
led1 = LED(4)
led2 = LED(17)
while True:
    led1.on()
    led2.on()
    led1.off()
    led2.off()
```

Instead of turning on and off together, on a Pi Zero there is a delay of about 140μs:

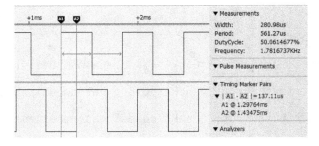

On a Pi 4 the delay is 10μs and on a Pi 5 it is 20μs:

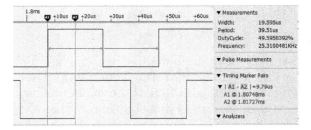

The difference between 20μs and 140μs might not seem like much - and for an LED, you would be hard pressed to notice that they weren't coming on at the same time. However, if you switch ten LEDs on and off the time difference from the first to the last would be about 1.5ms for the Pi Zero, which might be noticeable as a flicker.

There are also situations when you are driving a device in which you need one or more signals to have a fixed and exact phase relationship – one on while the other is off, say. The best known example of this is motor direction control. This is usually achieved using a configuration known as an H-bridge, see Chapter 11, which has two control lines. Activating one line at a time makes the motor turn in two different directions whereas activating them both at the same time shorts the power supply out and causes damage. If both of these lines are driven by a GPIO line then there will be a short time – $10\mu s$ to $150\mu s$ – when both lines are active. The result is that the power supply is short circuited for this time and in most cases damage accumulates over time.

You cannot assume that things happen at the same time. In fact, it is the rule that things do not happen at the same time unless you go to the trouble to make sure they do.

Summary

- From the programming point of view, there are only two simple on/off devices, LED and Buzzer. They both inherit from DigitalOutputDevice.

- The blink method turns the device on and off a given number of times and can be run in the background while the program gets on with something else or in the foreground when your program will wait.

- The toggle method turns the device on if it is off and off if it is on.

- The Buzzer class is intended to be used with a piezoelectric buzzer, which is either on or off and hence either emits a sound or remains silent. It can only make one tone, which cannot be varied.

- A piezo buzzer doesn't need a driver as it takes very little current.

- You can create a custom on/off device by inheriting from DigitalOutputDevice and providing the additional methods that are required. Restricting access to any existing inappropriate methods is a more difficult task.

- You can switch multiple on/off devices at the same time or at coordinated times, but there is always a lag between switching devices - $140\mu s$ for a Pi Zero and $10\mu s$ to $20\mu s$ for a Pi 4/5.

Chapter 6
Pins And Pin Factories

GPIO Zero is built on top of existing software libraries to the Pi's hardware – to the GPIO lines hence GPIO libraries. You can use these libraries directly but they generally work in C and are not easy to get to grips with. To make things easier the GPIO libraries are wrapped by GPIO Zero Python classes, the pin factories. Their purpose is not only to create pin objects with the characteristics you specify, but to also manage the use of GPIO lines, ensuring that you cannot use the same GPIO line for two different purposes at the same time, and to provide a certain amount of event handling.

The reason pin factories are needed is that they cover up the differences between the different GPIO libraries and present a single uniform Pin object no matter which library you chose to use.

That is, in GPIO Zero a Pin object allows you to work directly with a GPIO line in the same way irrespective of the GPIO library in use.

As GPIO Zero selects a default pin factory you can mostly ignore the whole issue of pin factories and pins until you need to do something that goes outside of the box. So first let's look at how to use a Pin object.

Raw GPIO Pin

In the Blinky program we used an LED object to turn the LED on and off – why not just reference the GPIO line? In other words, why hide the fact that we are working with GPIO lines? The answer is that it makes it easier to read programs. If you want to work with the raw GPIO line you can, but it isn't as clear what the program means, i.e. what is the GPIO line controlling.

To use a pin from the pin factory that GPIO Zero has set up for you all you have to do is create a pin, set its function as 'input' or 'output' and then use it. For example, the pin equivalent of the blinking LED program is:

```
from gpiozero import Device
from time import sleep
Device()
pin=Device.pin_factory.pin(4)
pin._set_function('output')
while True:
    pin.state=1
    sleep(1)
    pin.state=0
    sleep(1)
```

Notice that you have to have a call to the `Device` constructor to initialize the `pin_factory` before you can use it. The pin factory creates a pin object for GPIO4 and then we use its methods to control what it does.

All pin objects have three fundamental methods:

```
_get_function
_set_function
_get_state
```

There is also a set of optional get/set methods which in practice all pin objects support. These methods are grouped together to implement properties:

Function	Input/Output
`state`	0/1
`pull`	Up/down/floating see next chapter
`frequency`	Frequency of output/none
`bounce`	Time in seconds/none, see Chapter 7
`edge`	Rising/falling/both/none, see Chapter 8
`when_changed`	Function called when an edge event occurs

There are also three general methods:

`close`	Releases pin and cleans up
`output_with_state`	Sets pin to output and given state
`input_with_pull`	Set pin to input with given pull, see Chapter 7

The output_with_state is useful because it sets the initial state of the GPIO line, i.e. where things start from. For example:

```
pin._set_function('output',1)
```

sets the pin to output and high.

You would probably agree that `LED.on()` is easier to understand than `pin._set_state(1)`, but it isn't a huge difference.

GPIO Zero uses the `Pin` class to build easier-to-use classes that implement the functionality of real devices like LEDs. Later this idea becomes even more useful as the `Pin` class is used to build more complicated devices that make use of multiple GPIO lines.

You may notice that the pin's methods start with an underscore which is the usual way of indicating that a method is private and should not be used. This is because the `Pin` class is intended to be used as the basis for other classes like `LED` and so on, rather than being used directly. Later we will discover how to use it to create new, higher-level, classes similar to `LED`. That is, if you want to add a new device to GPIO Zero then at first you might use the `Pin` class to get a prototype working, but after this stage you should rewrite the code so that the pins are hidden and the object works in more natural terms. For example, if you have a new gas sensor you might first use `pin` objects to get it working, but the final `Gas` object would have methods like get_reading, calibrate and so on with no mention of GPIO lines at all.

Which Pin Factory?

If you are happy with the default pin factory there is no need to get deeply involved in selecting a pin factory and you can skip this section and return to it if you ever need to find out more.

The lower-level GPIO libraries interact directly with the hardware and as such they have to be written to work with specific versions of the Pi. Until the Pi 5 this wasn't difficult as the GPIO implementation was fairly standard. The Pi 5 implements GPIO and other I/O in a new way and this means that the existing GPIO libraries don't work with it. At the time of writing the only way of using the GPIO and other I/O in the same way across all version of the Pi is to use Linux drivers. The Linux drivers are uniform across all versions of the Pi and this is why they make a good foundation for the default `LGPIOFactory`. The problem is that Linux drivers tend to be slow and there are faster pin libraries. Indeed, speed is about the only good reason for using something other than the default.

If GPIO Zero is let down by anything, it is the lack of a really high quality high speed GPIO library that works across all versions of the Pi to base a pin factory on. As a result each of the alternative pin factories have advantages and disadvantages.

For GPIO Zero 2 the default pin factory was changed to be `LGPIOFactory`, which is currently the only factory that works on all versions of the Pi, including the Pi 5. In principle, it should work on any Linux-based system as it uses the standard `gpiochip` devices. For this reason it is advised that you use the default pin factory unless you have a good reason not to.

Before GPIO Zero 2 the default pin factory, and hence the most commonly used, was `RpiGPIOFactory`. However, it doesn't work on the Pi 5 nor does it support the SPI bus, I2C, hardware pulse width modulation (PWM) or the 1-wire bus. It also isn't undergoing much development and so these features are unlikely to be added in the future. It is faster than the new default pin factory and as such is sometimes worth using in its place if you are sure that you don't need your program to work on a Pi 5.

The other alternative pin factories are mostly only of historical interest and are included here in case you have to deal with some old software that makes use of them.

RPIOFactory is faster, doesn't load the CPU and supports a clever software implementation of PWM using DMA (Direct Memory Access), but it doesn't support the Pi 5, Pi 4 or the Pi Zero and it is no longer supplied as part of GPIO Zero 2. No work has been done on the project since 2014 and the project's GitHub page notes that it is no longer maintained and is looking for a new maintainer.

The pigpio library also uses DMA to create software PWM on any line, but it currently has only experimental support for the Pi 4 and no support for the Pi 5. Its use of a daemon to control the GPIO lines also seems to have some stability problems. However, the project is still on-going and, if you are prepared for slightly more complexity, it is worth trying. This pin factory is also the only one that supports remote GPIO. It does at least seem to be a well-implemented current project.

The final choice is NativeFactory which is completely Python-based. You can read the code to see how it works and it is very educational. Sadly, it isn't fully implemented and, while it supports the SPI bus in hardware and software, it doesn't support PWM at all.

There is also MockFactory which creates software pins that can be used for testing when a Pi isn't available.

To summarize:

For most applications the default LGPIOFactory is the best choice simply because it is the default, supports all version of the Pi including the Pi 5 and is likely to be the one supported in the future. Its only disadvantage is that it is slower than some alternatives.

The only other pin factory worth considering is the RpiGPIOFactory which is faster but it doesn't run on the Pi 5 and isn't likely to see much development in the future.

Currently LGPIOFactory has no ability to work with I2C or 1-wire devices. For these you need to work directly with Linux Drivers as explained in *Raspberry Pi IOT in Python with Linux Drivers*, ISBN:9781871962659.

Setting a Pin Factory

If you don't bother to specify a pin factory, GPIO Zero will try to locate one for you and if it can't find one, because none are installed, it will use the `NativeFactory` which is always available. In most cases this means that `LGPIOFactory` will be used as it is installed by default.

You can also set the pin factory to use on the command line using the `export` command:

```
export GPIOZERO_PIN_FACTORY = name of pin Factory
```

You can explicitly select a pin factory from within Python by setting `Device.pin_factory`:

```
Device.pin_factory = factoryClass()
```

where `factoryClass` is the name for the factory as listed in the table below.

You can also read `Device.pin_factory` to discover which pin factory is in use.

Each pin factory generates a pin class with a specific name but these all work in the same way and have the same methods and properties. Wbat this means is that you can treat pins produced by any pin factory in the same way.

The Factory and Pin classes corresponding to each of the options are:

Name	Factory class	Pin class
lgpio	gpiozero.pins.lgpio.LGPIOFactory	gpiozero.pins.lgpio.LGPIOPin
rpigpio	gpiozero.pins.rpigpio.RPiGPIOFactory	gpiozero.pins.rpigpio.RPiGPIOPin
pigpio	gpiozero.pins.pigpio.PiGPIOFactory	gpiozero.pins.pigpio.PiGPIOPin
native	gpiozero.pins.native.NativeFactory	gpiozero.pins.native.NativePin

You can also specify the pin factory as a parameter in each device constructor:

```
LED(7,pin_factory=factoryClass())
```

However, this approach has little value and you should only ever use a single pin factory in a given program. The best advice is to ignore the `pin_factory` parameter unless you have a good reason not to. Set the pin factory at the start of your program and don't change it.

You can also create and use a pin factory object directly:

```
from gpiozero.pins.native import NativeFactory
myFactory = NativeFactory()

pin = myFactory.pin(4)
```

How Fast?

A key question for any IoT system is how fast can it operate? In this context we need a rough idea how fast GPIO Zero can toggle GPIO lines. Notice that this question depends not just on GPIO Zero, but also on the pin factory in use. For simplicity, we will look at only lgpio, the default and rpigpio, the previous default.

We can answer this question immediately with a simple program:

```
from gpiozero import LED
led = LED(4)
while True:
    led.on()
    led.off()
```

If you run this on a Pi Zero using rpigpio, which is the fastest pin factory, the output is 3.6kHz, which means you can switch an LED on for $136\mu s$. For a Pi 4 the output is 51kHz and just short of $10\mu s$. In other words, the Pi 4 is around ten times faster.

As LGPIOFactory is the only pin factory that works with the Pi 5 we cannot try this with rpigpio, but the same program, using lgpio, produces $20\mu s$ pulses with a frequency of 24kHz.

You might think that an apparently simpler program:

```
from gpiozero import LED
led = LED(4)
while True:
    led.toggle()
```

would get the job done faster, but no. The toggle operation is more complex and the toggle method simply hides this. In this case a Pi Zero runs at 1.8kHz and a Pi 4 at 24kHz, i.e. this method takes twice as long.

What about working with the pin directly? This should be faster as it avoids using additional code in GPIO Zero. Using the default pin factory:

```
from gpiozero import Device
Device()
pin = Device.pin_factory.pin(4)
pin._set_function("output")
while True:
    pin.state=1
    pin.state=0
```

If you try this out using rpigpio on a Pi Zero you will find that you get 25kHz and on a Pi 4 300kHz, i.e. more than ten times faster than using the LED object. Different pin factories will give you different upper limits, but the speed increase using the pin object directly should be similar. On a Pi 5, the frequency is 38kHz, which is a consequence of the LGPIOFactory being about ten times slower than rpigpio.

Roughly speaking, GPIO Zero running on a Pi Zero with `rpigpio` is of the order of 100μs to 20μs and on a Pi 4 10μs to 3μs is its characteristic time. On a Pi 5 with `LGPIOFactory` the characteristic time is 40μs to 20μs. On the same machine `rpigio` is about ten time faster than `LGPIOFactory`.

Compare this to the same task programmed directly in C, which has a characteristic time of around 0.01us, i.e. 10ns, i.e. at least 100 times faster than the fastest pin factory on a Pi 4 and 1000 times faster than `lgpio` on a Pi 5.

There is no doubt if you need speed for this sort of task then Python is not the language to use. C is a much better choice as outlined in *Raspberry Pi IoT in C, Second Edition,* ISBN:9781871962635. This said, there are many applications that operate at almost human timescales and for this Python is very adequate and much simpler. If you can, use Python and unless speed is an issue use the default pin factory.

The Problem of Clocks

Until relatively recently processors, and computer systems in general, used a very simple approach to clock frequencies. Each time a clock pulse occurs something happens in the system and, for simplicity, clocks were set to run at a fixed maximum rate that allowed the system to remain cool. Today's systems, however, make use of multiple clocks which run at variable rates. This allows a system to "sprint", i.e. use a higher clock rate for a short time, to keep the temperature increase below a set level. If the temperature increases too much then the clock can be throttled, i.e. slowed down, until the system is once again within a safe zone. Slowing the clock can also be used to reduce power consumption.

A variable clock rate is good from the point of view of completing tasks, and perhaps reducing power consumption, but if you are trying to write programs where timing is critical it can be a problem. If you synchronize your program using a known change in a timer, which always ticks at the same rate irrespective of the system clock, then your program will work in the same way irrespective of the speed of the system clock. However, this is not true if the system clock runs so slow that the program cannot complete the task in the allotted time.

The latest version of Pi OS implements the Linux `cpufreq` kernel driver, but things are more complicated with the Pi because it is the GPU that controls things, not the CPU. You can find out what the GPU is doing using the `vcgencmd` command, which talks directly to the GPU, whereas the standard Linux commands work with the CPU and sometimes give the wrong answer.

The `vcgencmd` is fully documented at the official site, but the important command for clock speed is:

```
vcgencmd measure_clock arm
```

You can substitute other clock names for `arm`, but this gives you the frequency that all of the cores are running at.

The Linux `cpufreq` commands are standard, but in some situations the GPU may change the clock frequency without Linux being aware of it. The idea is that there are a set of "governors" that control how the frequency is varied. For the current generation of Pis the default is `ondemand`, but you can find which the current active governor is using:

```
sudo cat /sys/devices/system/cpu/cpu0/cpufreq/scaling_governor
```

and you can find out the available governors using:

```
sudo cat
/sys/devices/system/cpu/cpu0/cpufreq/scaling_available_governors
```

The action of the `ondemand` governor according to the Linux manual is:

> *The cpufreq governor "ondemand" sets the CPU frequency depending on the current system load. Load estimation is triggered by the scheduler through the update_util_data->func hook; when triggered, cpufreq checks the CPU-usage statistics over the last period and the governor sets the CPU accordingly.*

Setting the frequency on the basis of load makes sense for many applications, but for an IoT app that needs high speed, even though it doesn't load the CPU, it isn't ideal.

Empirically, the Pi Zero seems to regard its single core as being heavily loaded all of the time as it always reports 1GHz as its clock rate, but the Pi 4 reports it as low as 600MHz given a low load. You can discover the current clock rate according to Linux and the max and min frequencies used using:

```
cat /sys/devices/system/cpu/cpu0/cpufreq/scaling_cur_freq
cat /sys/devices/system/cpu/cpu0/cpufreq/scaling_min_freq
cat /sys/devices/system/cpu/cpu0/cpufreq/scaling_max_freq
```

For the Pi Zero the maximum frequency is 1GHz, for the Pi 4 it is 1.5GHz and for the Pi 5 it is 2.4GHz

If you need a fixed clock frequency you have to set the governor to a performance which sets the clock to the highest possible frequency, usually scaling_max_freq:

```
sudo sh -c "echo performance >
    /sys/devices/system/cpu/cpu0/cpufreq/scaling_governor"
```

This will run the clock at the highest frequency, but if the CPU temperature goes over the maximum the frequency will still be reduced.

In most cases, you can ignore clock speed variation with load, but you do need to keep the effect in mind when searching for explanations of why things aren't happening as fast as you might expect.

Summary

- GPIO Zero uses the idea of a pin factory to allow a variety of direct interfaces with the GPIO lines to be used.

- You should select a single pin factory to be used at the start of your program and not change it.

- The default pin factory, lgpio, is installed by default and is currently the best choice.

- The previous default pin factory rpigpio is about ten times faster than lgpio but it doesn't work on the Pi 5.

- In most cases, pin objects are constructed by the devices you use such as LEDs and you don't have to interact with the pin factory at all.

- You can use the pin factory directly to obtain a pin object and work with this directly

- Working directly with a pin object is approximately ten times faster than working with it via a device-derived class.

- Modern Pis have a variable rate clock, which can be a problem when you are trying to run IoT programs at the fastest speed irrespective of what the CPU load is.

- You can use operating system commands to set the speed governor to a fixed speed, usually the maximum possible. However, CPU over-temperature events will still reduce the clock speed as a safety precaution.

Chapter 7

Some Electronics

Now that we have looked at some simple I/O, it is worth spending a little time on the electronics of output and input.

First some basic electronics – how transistors can be used as switches. The approach is very simple, but it is enough for the simple circuits that digital electronics makes use of. It isn't enough to design a high quality audio amplifier or similar analog device, but it might be all you need.

The basis of all electronics is Ohm's law, $V = IR$, and this prerequisite implies an understanding of voltage, current and resistance.

How to Think About Circuits

For a beginner electronics can seem very abstract, but that's not how old hands think about it. Most understand what is going on in terms of a hydraulic model, even if they don't admit it. The basic idea is that an electric current running in a wire is very much like a flow of water in a pipe. The source of the electricity plays the role of a pump and the wires, the pipe. The flow of electricity is measured in Amps and this is just the amount of electricity that flows per second. The flow is governed by how hard the pump is pumping, which is measured by voltage and how restrictive the pipe is, the resistance which is measured in Ohms.

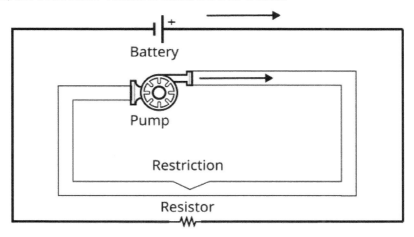

It is true that when you are doing electronics you are basically doing plumbing with a fluid that you generally can't see that flows in pipes called wires.

The only difficult one of these three ideas is the idea of pumping force. We tend to think of a pump providing a flow at the location of the pump but there is something, "a pumping force" that keeps the water flowing around every part of the circuit. In your imagination you have to think of the water being forced ever onward at every point in the pipe. In particular when there is constriction in the pipe then you might need more pumping force to get the water through. In a sense the pump provides the total pressure available and this distributes itself around the circuit as needed to push the flow through each restriction.

In electric circuits the pumping force is called EMF or Electro Motive Force or just voltage. We also assume that the force needed to push electricity through wires is negligible and resistors are the only place that a voltage is needed to make the current flow.

The relationship between these quantities is characterized by Ohm's law:

$V = IR$ or $I = V/R$ or $R = V/I$

where V is the voltage in Volts, I is the current in Amps and R is the resistance in Ohms.

It is worth pointing out that we generally work in Volts (V) and milliamps (mA), one thousandth of an amp, in Ohm's law and this automatically gives resistance in kilo-ohms (kΩ).

You can see that if you increase the voltage, the flow, then the current increases. If you increase the resistance then the current decreases. Slightly more difficult is the idea that for a given resistance you need particular pumping force to achieve a given flow. If you know the actual flow and the resistance then you can work out the pumping force needed to get that flow.

The following points should be obvious. The flow through a pipe has to be the same at each point in the pipe – otherwise water would backup or need to be introduced. The total pressure that the pump provides has to be distributed across each of the resistances in the pipe to ensure the same flow. These pressures have to add up to the total pressure that the pump provides.

Slightly less obvious, but you can still understand them in terms of water flow, pressures add, currents add and resistances to flow in the same pipe add.

One of the main reasons for understanding electrical flow is that you can use Ohm's law to avoid damaging things. As a current flows through a resistor it gets hot. The rule here is that the energy produced is proportional to VI. If you double the current, you double the heating effect. Most electronic devices have current limits beyond which they are liable to fail. One of the basic tasks in designing any electronic circuit is to work out what the current is and, if it is too high, add a resistor or lower the voltage to reduce it. To do this you need a good understanding of the hydraulic model and be able to use Ohm's law. There are examples later in this chapter.

It is also worth pointing out that there are devices which do not obey Ohm's law – so called non-Ohmic devices. These are the interesting elements in a circuit – LEDs, diodes, transistors and so on, but even these devices can be understood in terms of the flow of a fluid.

This is a lightning introduction to electronics, pun intended, and there is much to learn and many mistakes to make, most of which result in blue smoke.

Electrical Drive Characteristics

If you are not very familiar with electronics the important things to know are what voltages are being worked with and how much current can flow. The most important thing to know about the Pi is that it works with two voltage levels – 0V and 3.3V. If you have worked with other logic devices you might be more familiar with 0V and 5V as being the low and high levels. The Pi uses a lower output voltage to reduce its power consumption, which is beneficial, but you need to keep in mind that you may have to use some electronics to convert the 3.3V to other values. The same is true of inputs, which must not exceed 3.3V or you risk damaging the Pi.

In output mode a single GPIO line can source and sink 16mA, but the situation is a little more complicated than this suggests.

Unfortunately, the Pi power supply can only supply enough power for all of the GPIO lines working at around 3mA each. If you use too much current then the 3.3V supply will fail. The safe limit is usually stated as 50mA in total, i.e all of the GPIO lines have to keep their current consumption below a total of 50mA. When you get close to this limit you might find that current spikes cause strange behavior. In addition, no single GPIO line should supply or sink more than 8mA, or 16mA if you configure a high drive current, see later.

In practice, if you are planning to use more than 3mA from multiple GPIO lines, consider using a transistor. If your circuits draw more than 50mA from the 3.3V supply rail, consider a separate power supply. You can use the 5V supply with a regulator if you need even more 3.3V supply current. How much current the 5V pin can source is a difficult question that depends on the USB power supply in use, but 2A is a reasonable estimate if there are no other USB devices connected. The total of all USB, HDMI, Camera, and 5V pins has to be less than 2.5A. If in doubt use a separate power supply.

Notice that the 16mA limit means that you cannot safely drive a standard 20mA red LED without restricting the current to below 16mA. A better solution is to use a low-power 2mA LED or use a transistor driver.

Driving an LED

One of the first things you need to know how to do is compute the value of a current-limiting resistor. For example, if you just connect an LED across a GPIO line and ground then no current will flow when the line is low and the LED is off, but when the line is high at 3.3V it is highly likely that the current will exceed the safe limit. In most cases nothing terrible will happen as the Pi's GPIO lines are rated very conservatively, but if you keep doing it eventually something will fail. The correct thing to do is to use a current-limiting resistor.

Although this is an essential part of using an LED, it is also something you need to keep in mind when connecting any output device. You need to discover the voltage that the device needs and the current it uses and calculate a current-limiting resistor to make sure that is indeed the current it draws from the GPIO line.

An LED is a non-linear electronic component – the voltage across it stays more or less the same irrespective of the current passing through the device. Compare this to a more normal linear, or "Ohmic", device where the current and voltage vary together according to Ohm's law, $V = IR$, which means that if the current doubles, so does the voltage.

This is not how an LED behaves. It has a fairly constant voltage drop irrespective of the current. (If you are curious, the relationship between current and voltage for an LED is exponential, meaning that big changes in the current hardly change the voltage across the LED.) When you use an LED you need to look up its forward voltage drop, about 1.7V to 2V for a red LED and about 3V for a blue LED, and the maximum current, usually 20mA for small LEDs. You don't have to use the current specified, this is the maximum current and maximum brightness.

To work out the current-limiting resistor you simply calculate the voltage across the resistor and then use Ohm's law to give you the resistor you need for the current required. The LED determines the voltage and the resistor sets the current.

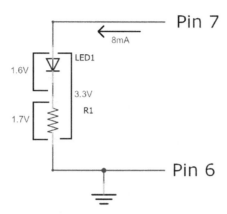

A GPIO line supplies 3.3V and if you assume 1.6V, its forward voltage, across the LED that leaves 1.7V across the current-limiting resistor since voltage distributes itself across components connected in series. If we restrict the current to 8mA, which is very conservative, then the resistor we need is given by:

R = V/I = 1.7/8 = 0.212

The result is in kiloOhms, kΩ, because the current is in milliamps, mA. So we need at least a 212Ω resistor. In practice, you can use a range of values as long as the resistor is around 200Ω – the bigger the resistor the smaller the current, but the dimmer the LED. If you were using multiple GPIO lines then keeping the current down to 3mA would be better, but that would need a transistor.

You need to do this sort of calculation when driving other types of output devices. The steps are always the same. The 3.3V distributes itself across the output device and the resistor in some proportion and we know the maximum current – from these values we can compute the resistor needed to keep the actual current below this value.

LED BJT Drive

Often you need to reduce the current drawn from a GPIO line and for this you can use a Bipolar Junction Transistor (BJT), a current amplifier which is low in cost and easy to use.

A BJT is a three-terminal device - base, emitter and collector - in which the current that flows through the emitter/collector is controlled by the current in the base:

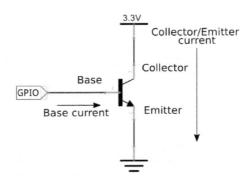

The diagram shows an NPN transistor, which is the most common type. This diagram is a simplification in that, in reality, the current in the emitter is slightly larger than that in the collector because you have to add the current flowing in the base.

In most cases, all you have to know are two additional facts. Firstly, the voltage on the base is approximately 0.6V, no matter how much current flows since the base is a diode, a nonlinear device just like the LED in the previous section. Secondly, the current in the collector/emitter is hfe or ß (beta) times the current in the base. That is, hfe or beta is the current gain of the transistor and you look it up for any transistor you want to use. While you are consulting the data sheets, you also need to check the maximum currents and voltages the device will tolerate. In most cases, the beta is between 100 and 200 and hence you can use a transistor to amplify the GPIO current by at least a factor of 100.

Notice that, for the emitter/collector current to be non-zero, the base has to have a current flowing into it. If the base is connected to ground then the transistor is "cut off", i.e. no current flows. What this means is that when the GPIO line is high the transistor is "on" and current is flowing and when the GPIO line is low the transistor is "off" and no current flows.

This high-on/low-off behavior is typical of an NPN transistor. A PNP transistor works the other way round:

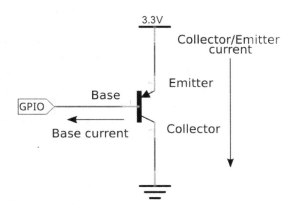

The 0.6V is between the base and the collector and the current flows out of the base. What this means is that the transistor is off when the GPIO line is high and on when it is low.

This complementary behavior of NPN and PNP BJTs is very useful and means that we can use such transistors in pairs. It is also worth knowing that the diagram given above is usually drawn with 0V at the top of the diagram, i.e. flipped vertically, to make it look the same as the NPN diagram. Always make sure you know where the +V line is.

A BJT Example

For a simple example we need to connect a standard LED to a GPIO line with a full 20mA drive. Given that all of the Pi's GPIO lines work at 3.3V and ideally only supply a few milliamps, we need a transistor to drive the LED which typically draws 20mA.

You could use a Field Effect Transistor (FET) of some sort, but for this sort of application a BJT works very well and is available in a thru-hole mount, i.e. it comes with wires.

Almost any general purpose NPN transistor will work, but the 2N2222 is very common. From its data sheet, you can discover that the max collector current is 800mA and beta is at least 50 which makes it suitable for driving a 20mA LED with a GPIO current of at most 20/50mA = 0.4mA.

The circuit is simple but we need two current-limiting resistors:

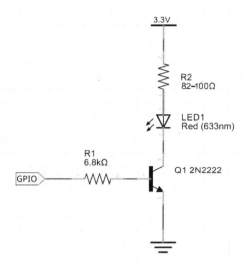

If you connected the base to the GPIO line directly then the current flowing in the base would be unrestricted – it would be similar to connecting the GPIO line to ground. R1 restricts the current to 0.39mA, which is very low and, assuming that the transistor has a minimum gain (hfe) of 50, this provides just short of 20mA to power it.

The calculation is that the GPIO supplies 3.3V and the base has 0.6V across it so the voltage across R1 is 3.3 - 0.6V = 2.7V. To limit the current to 0.4mA would need a resistor of $2.7/0.4k\Omega = 6.7k\Omega$. The closest preferred value is $6.8k\Omega$ which gives a slightly smaller current.

Without R2 the LED would draw a very large current and burn out. R2 limits the current to 20mA. Assuming a forward voltage drop of 1.6V and a current of 20mA the resistor is given by $(3.3-1.6)/20k\Omega = 85\Omega$. In practice, we could use anything in the range 82Ω to 100Ω.

The calculation just given assumes that the voltage between the collector and emitter is zero, but of course in practice it isn't. Ignoring this results in a current less than 20mA, which is erring on the safe side. The data sheet indicates that the collector emitter voltage is less than 200mV.

The point is that you rarely make exact calculations for circuits such as this, you simply arrive at acceptable and safe operating conditions. You can also use this design to drive something that needs a higher voltage. For example, to drive a 5V dip relay, which needs 10mA to activate it, you would use something like:

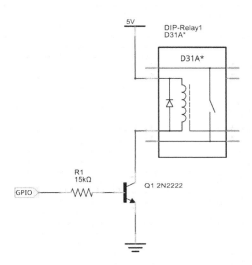

Notice that in this case the transistor isn't needed to increase the drive current – the GPIO line could provide the 10mA directly. Its purpose is to change the voltage from 3.3V to 5V. The same idea works with any larger voltage.

If you are using the 2N2222 then the pinouts are:

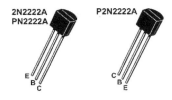

As always, the positive terminal on the LED is the long pin.

MOSFET Driver

There are many who think that the FET (Field Effect Transistor), or more precisely the MOSFET (Metal Oxide Semiconductor FET), is the perfect amplification device and we should ignore BJTs. They are simpler to understand and use, but it can be more difficult to find one with the characteristics you require.

Like the BJT, a MOSFET has three terminals called the gate, drain and source. The current that you want to control flows between the source and drain and it is controlled by the gate. This is analogous to the BJT's base, collector and emitter, but the difference is that it is the voltage on the gate that controls the current between the source and drain.

The gate is essentially a high resistance input and very little current flows in it. This makes it an ideal way to connect a GPIO line to a device that needs more current or a different voltage. When the gate voltage is low the source drain current is very small. When the gate voltage reaches the threshold voltage $V_{GS(th)}$, which is different for different MOSFETs, the source drain current starts to increase exponentially. Basically when the gate is connected to 0V or below $V_{GS(th)}$ the MOSFET is off and when it is above $V_{GS(th)}$ the MOSFET starts to turn on. Don't think of $V_{GS(th)}$ as the gate voltage at which the MOSFET turns on, but as the voltage below which it is turned off. The problem is that the gate voltage to turn a typical MOSFET fully on is in the region of 10V. Special "logic" MOSFETs need a gate voltage around 5V to fully turn on and this makes the 3.3V at which the Raspberry Pi's GPIO lines work a problem. The data sheets usually give the fully on resistance and the minimum gate voltage that produces it, usually listed as Drain-Source On-State Resistance. For digital work this is a more important parameter than the gate threshold voltage.

You can deal with this problem in one of two ways – ignore it or find a MOSFET with a very small $V_{GS(th)}$. In practice, MOSFETs with thresholds low enough to work at 3.3V are hard to find and when you do find them they are generally only available as surface mount. Ignoring the problem sometimes works if you can tolerate the MOSFET not being fully on. If the current is kept low then, even though the MOSFET might have a resistance of a few Ohms, the power loss and voltage drop may be acceptable.

What MOSFETs are useful for is in connecting higher voltages to a GPIO line used as an input, see later.

Also notice that this discussion has been in terms of an N-channel MOSFET. A P-channel works in the same way, but with all polarities reversed. It is cut off when the gate is at the positive voltage and turns on when the gate is grounded. This is exactly the same as the NPN versus PNP for the BJT.

MOSFET LED

A BJT is the easiest way to drive an LED, but as an example of using a common MOSFET we can arrange to drive one using a 2N7000, a low-cost, N-channel device available in a standard TO92 form factor suitable for experimentation:

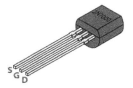

Its data sheet states that it has a $V_{GS(th)}$ of typically 2V, but it could be as low as 0.8V or as high as 3V. Given we are trying to work with a gate voltage of 3.3V you can see that in the worst case this is hardly going to work – the device will only just turn on. The best you can do is to buy a batch of 2N7000 and measure their $V_{GS(th)}$ to weed out any that are too high. This said, the circuit given below does generally work.

Assuming a $V_{GS(th)}$ of 2V and a current of 20mA for the LED, the data sheet gives a rough value of 6Ω for the on resistance with a gate voltage of 3V. The calculation for the current-limiting resistor is the same as in the BJT case and the final circuit is:

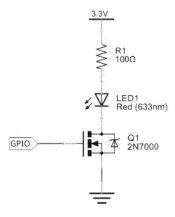

Notice that we don't need a current-limiting resistor for the GPIO line as the gate connection is high impedance and doesn't draw much current. In practice, it is usually a good idea to include a current-limiting resistor in the GPIO line if you plan to switch it on and off rapidly. The problem is that the gate looks like a capacitor and fast changes in voltage can produce high currents. While there could be devices labeled 2N7000 that will not work in this circuit due to the threshold gate voltage being too high, encountering one is rare.

A logic-level MOSFET like the IRLZ44 has a resistance of 0.028Ω at 5V compared to the 2N2222's of 6Ω. It also has a $V_{GS(th)}$ guaranteed to be between 1V and 2V.

Setting Drive Type

The GPIO output can be configured into one of a number of modes, but the most important is pull-up/down. Before we get to the code to do the job, it is worth spending a moment explaining the three basic output modes, push-pull, pull-up and pull-down.

Push-Pull Mode

In push-pull mode two transistors of opposite polarity, one PNP and one NPN, are used:

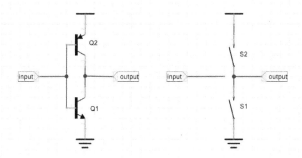

The circuit behaves like the two-switch equivalent shown on the right. Only one of the transistors, or switches, is "closed" at any time. If the input is high then Q1 is saturated and the output is connected to ground - exactly as if S1 was closed. If the input is low then Q2 is saturated, as if S2 was closed, and the output is connected to 3.3V. You can see that this pushes the output line high with the same "force" as it pulls it low. This is the standard configuration for a GPIO output.

Pull-Up Mode

In pull-up mode one of the transistors is replaced by a resistor:

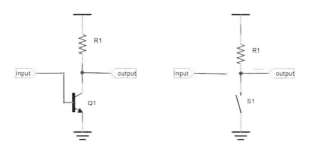

In this case the circuit is equivalent to having a single switch. When the switch is closed, the output line is connected to ground and hence driven low. When the switch is open, the output line is pulled high by the resistor. You can see that in this case the degree of pull-down is greater than the pull-up, where the current is limited by the resistor. The advantage of this mode is that it can be used in an AND configuration. If multiple GPIO or other lines are connected to the output, then any one of them being low will pull the output line low. Only when all of them are off does the resistor succeed in pulling the line high. This is used, for example, in a serial bus configuration like the SPI bus.

Pull-Down Mode

Finally, pull-down mode, which is the best mode for driving general loads, motors, LEDs, etc, is exactly the same as pull-up only now the resistor is used to pull the output line low.

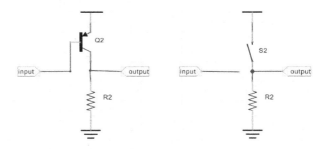

The line is held high by the transistor and pulled low by the resistor only when all the switches are open. Putting this the other way round, the line is high if any one switch is closed. This is the OR version of the shared bus idea.

Basic Input Circuit - The Switch

Now it is time to turn our attention to the electrical characteristics of GPIO lines as inputs. One of the most common input circuits is the switch or button. Many beginners make the mistake of wiring a GPIO line to a switch something like:

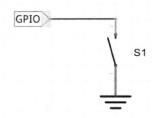

The problem with this is that, if the switch is pressed, the GPIO line is connected to ground and will read as zero. The question is, what does it read when the switch is open? A GPIO line configured as an input has a very high resistance. It isn't connected to any particular voltage and the voltage on it varies due to the static it picks up. The jargon is that the unconnected line is "floating". When the switch is open the line is floating and, if you read it, the result, zero or one, depends on whatever noise it has picked up.

The correct way to do the job is to tie the input line either high or low when the switch is open using a resistor. A pull-up arrangement would be something like:

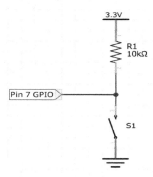

The value of the resistor used isn't critical. It simply pulls the GPIO line high when the switch isn't pressed. When it is pressed a current of a little more than 0.3mA flows in the resistor. If this is too much increase the resistance to 100kΩ or even more - but notice that the higher the resistor value the noisier the input to the GPIO and the more it is susceptible to RF interference. Notice that this gives a zero when the switch is pressed.

If you want a switch that pulls the line high instead of low, reverse the logic by swapping the positions of the resistor and the switch in the diagram to create a pull-down:

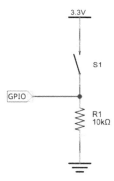

Notice that this gives a one when the switch is pressed.

The good news is that the Raspberry Pi has built-in pull-up and pull-down resistors which you can enable in software. This means that you can connect a switch directly to the GPIO and set a pull-up or pull-down configuration in software.

Setting Pull Mode

The GPIO Zero library makes it easy to set the pull mode as the pin object supports a pull property. You can set this to any of up, down or floating. In output mode floating is push-pull mode. For example:

```
pin.pull="down"
```

Any device that has a pin property can have its pull mode set in the same way and many devices include a pull parameter in their constructor. The internal pull-up/pull-down resistors are in the range 50kΩ to 65kΩ. There are also external 1.8kΩ pull-ups on pins 3 and 5. The only way to remove them is to unsolder them from the board.

Debounce

Although the switch is the simplest input device, it is very difficult to get right. When a user clicks a switch of any sort, the action isn't clean - the switch bounces. What this means is that the logic level on the GPIO line goes high then low and high again and bounces between the two until it settles down. There are electronic ways of debouncing switches, but software does the job much better. All you have to do is insert a delay of a millisecond or so after detecting a switch press and read the line again - if it is still low then record a switch press. Similarly, when the switch is released, read the state twice with a delay. You can vary the delay to modify the perceived characteristics of the switch.

A more sophisticated algorithm for debouncing a switch is based on the idea of integration. All you have to do is read the state multiple times, every few milliseconds say, and keep a running sum of values. If you sum ten values each time then a total of between 6 and 10 can be taken as an indication that the switch is high. A total less than this indicates that the switch is low. You can think of this as a majority vote in the time period for the switch being high or low.

GPIO Zero supports a simple debounce algorithm. After a change in the input has been detected, further changes are ignored for a period of time. You can set the debounce time using the bounce property. For example:

```
pin.bounce=5/1000
```

sets the bounce time to 5ms which is a reasonable choice for many devices. Notice that this means that the bounced switch can only be pressed and released 100 times a second. Input devices also often have bounce parameters that can be set in their constructors.

The Potential Divider

If you have an input that is outside of the range of 0V to 3.3V you can reduce it using a simple potential divider. In the diagram V is the input from the external logic and Vout is the connection to the GPIO input line:

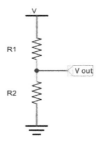

$$Vout = V \ R2/(R1+R2)$$

You can spend a lot of time working out good values of R1 and R2. For loads that take a lot of current you need R1+R2 to be small and divided in the same ratio as the voltages. For example, for a 5V device R1=18 or 20KΩ and R2=33KΩ work well to drop the voltage to 3.3V.

A simpler approach that works for a 5V signal is to notice that the ratio R1:R2 has to be the same as (5-3.3):3.3, i.e. the voltage divides itself across the resistors in proportion to their value, which is roughly 1:2. What this means is that you can take any resistor and use it for R1 and use two of the same value in series for R2 and the Vout will be 3.33333V.

The problem with a resistive divider is that it can round off fast pulses due to the small capacitive effects. This usually isn't a problem, but if it is then the solution is to use a FET or a BJT as an active buffer:

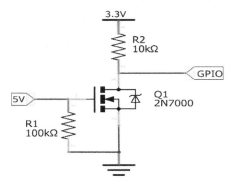

Notice that this is an inverting buffer, the output is low when the input is high, but you can usually ignore this and simply correct it in software, i.e. read a 1 as a low state and a 0 as a high state. The role of R1 is to make sure the FET is off when the 5V signal is absent and R2 limits the current in the FET to about 0.3mA.

In most cases you should try the simple voltage divider and only move to an active buffer if it doesn't work.

This very basic look at electronics isn't all that you need to know, but it is enough for you to see some of the problems and find some answers. In general, this sort of electronics is all about making sure that voltages and currents are within limits. As switching speeds increase you have additional problems, which are mainly concerned with making sure that your circuits aren't slowing things down. This is where things get more subtle.

Summary

- You can get a long way with only a small understanding of electronics, but you do need to know enough to protect the Pi and things you connect to it.

- The maximum current from any GPIO line should be less than 16mA and the total current should be less than 50mA.

- All of the GPIO lines work at 3.3V and you should avoid directly connecting any other voltage.

- You can drive an LED directly from a GPIO line, but only at 16mA rather than the nominal 20mA needed for full brightness.

- Calculating a current-limiting resistor always follows the same steps – find out the current in the device, find out the voltage across the device, and work out the resistor that supplies that current when the remainder of the voltage is applied to it.

- For any load you connect to a GPIO output you generally need a current-limiting resistor.

- In many cases you need a transistor, a BJT, to increase the current supplied by the GPIO line.

- To use a BJT you need to calculate a current-limiting resistor in the base and, generally, one in the collector.

- MOSFETs are popular alternatives to BJTs, but it is difficult to find a MOSFET that works reliably at 3.3V.

- GPIO output lines can be set to active push-pull mode, where a transistor is used to pull the line high or low, or passive pull-up or pull-down mode, where one transistor is used and a resistor pulls the line high or low when the transistor is inactive.

- GPIO lines have built-in pull-up and pull-down resistors which can be selected or disabled under software control and can be used in input mode.

- When used as inputs, GPIO lines have a very high resistance and in most cases you need pull-up or pull-down resistors to stop the line floating.

- The built-in pull-up or pull-down resistors can be used in input mode.

- Mechanical input devices have to be debounced to stop spurious input.

- If you need to connect an input to something bigger than 3.3V, you need a potential divider to reduce the voltage back to 3.3V. You can also use a transistor.

Chapter 8
Simple Input

GPIO input is a much more difficult problem than output from the point of view of measurement and verification. For output you can see the change in the signal on a logic analyzer and know the exact time that it occurred. This makes it possible to track down timing problems and fine-tune things with good accuracy. Input, on the other hand, is "silent" and unobservable. When did you read the status of the line? Usually the timing of the read is with respect to some other action that the device has taken. For example, you read the input line 20 μs after setting the output line high. In some applications the times are long and/or unimportant, but in some they are critical and so we need some strategies for monitoring and controlling read events.

The usual rule of thumb is to assume that it takes as long to read a GPIO line as it does to set it.

One common and very useful trick when you are trying to get the timing of input correct is to substitute an output command to a spare GPIO line and monitor it with a logic analyzer. Place the output instruction just before the input instruction and where you see the line change on the logic analyzer should be close to the time that the input would be read in the unmodified program. You can use this to debug and fine-tune and then remove the output statement.

The Button

The GPIO Zero library has only one simple input device – the Button, but for a simple input device it is surprisingly complicated. This is not its fault, but another reflection of the fact that input is hard.

Device ◄── GPIODevice ◄── InputDevice ◄── DigitalInputDevice ◄── Button

Of course, it doesn't have to be connected to a button - it can be any device that creates a definite high low signal on a GPIO line. The button could be any sort of switch that is actuated in any way – a reed switch activated by a magnet, a tilt switch activated by angle, and so on.

A reed switch is closed by being near a magnet.

A tilt switch is closed by being rotated until a blob of mercury makes a connection.

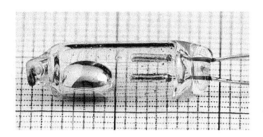

The `Button` has a surprising number of possible parameters:

```
Button(pin,pull_up=True, active_state=None, bounce_time=None,
                              hold_time=1, hold_repeat=False)
```

at its simplest, however, you only have to provide the pin number:

```
button = Button(4)
```

This puts the GPIO line, GPIO4 in this case, into input mode and the defaults are such that a pull-up is automatically used, see previous chapter. This means that you can wire a switch to GPIO4 without the need for any other components.

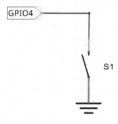

Ground is pin 6 and GPIO4 is pin 7.

If you want to use a pull-down arrangement, set `pull_up` to `False` when you create the pin.

The big question is, how do you deal with input from the switch? It isn't like output, where your program is in 100% control. The button can be pushed at any time and your program has to respond to it.

The simplest way of dealing with the problem is for your program to wait until the button is pressed or released:

```
wait_for_press(timeout = None)
wait_for_release(timeout = None)
```

The timeout can be set to the number of seconds to wait before giving up. The default value of `None` or `0` means your program will wait forever for the button to be pressed.

The use of press and release refer to the mechanical action of the button or switch. Of course, if the button is wired with a pull-up then press corresponds to a `0` and if it is wired as a pull-down then it corresponds to a `1`. To let the software know which is which, you can use the `active_state` parameter when creating the `Button` object. If you set this to `True` then high corresponds to pressed and if `False`, low corresponds to pressed. If `pull_up` is anything except `None`, `active_state` is set automatically.

By default `Button` isn't debounced. What this means is that what looks like a single press to you might be received as a set of press/release signals. If you don't want to incorporate hardware debounce components then include the `bounce_time` parameter when you create `button`. This specifies a wait time in seconds before its state change will be recognized. For example:

```
button = Button(4,bounce_time=0.25)
```

creates a Button that can only be pressed 4 times per second and hence is effectively debounced. Another way to look at this is that the button will only respond to the first press in any 0.25s interval.

Polling

The problem with waiting for a button, or whatever else you use as a switch, to be pressed is that your program is frozen and nothing else can happen - it just sits there waiting for the event. Sometimes this is acceptable because there is nothing more for your program to do. More often it is the case that your program has got things to do and simply waiting isn't an option.

An alternative to waiting for a switch to be pressed is to poll its state. Polling is a standard programming technique where, to detect a change of state, the program repeatedly checks the state at suitable intervals. You can check the state of `Button` using the `is_pressed` property or the `value` property. The difference is that `value` gives you the state of the GPIO line, i.e. `0` (low) or `1` (high) and what this means depends on the way the switch is wired, whereas `is_pressed` always gives `True` when the switch is pressed.

For example:

```
while True:
    do something
    if button.is_pressed:
        do something about button pressed
```

In this case the polling takes the form of an infinite loop and the test for the button being pressed occurs once per loop. You can see that how often the button press is tested depends on the time the loop takes and that how long the loop gets to *do something* depends on how often the button is pressed and how long it takes to process the changes needed.

The idea of using a polling loop is often regarded as a poor choice, but in practice it is generally the best choice as it uses the processor to respond as fast as possible to the button press while allowing it to get on with other tasks when it isn't. More sophisticated solutions, such as using an interrupt or event are often just a way of hiding a polling loop and tend to increase inefficiency. Polling loops are generally the best solution, but GPIO Zero does provide an alternative in the form of events.

Events and Interrupts

Interrupts and events do make some aspects of IoT programming easier, if not more efficient. But first what are interrupts and events?
An event is like a latch or a memory that something happened. Imagine that there is a flag that will be automatically set when an input line changes state. The flag is set without the involvement of software, or at least any software that you have control over. It is useful to imagine an entirely hardware-based setting of the flag, even if this is not always the case. With the help of an event, you can avoid missing an input because the polling loop was busy doing something else. Now the polling loop reads the flag rather than the actual state of the input line and hence it can detect if the line has changed since it was last polled. The polling loop resets the event flag and processes the event. Of course, it can't always know exactly when the event happened, but at least it hasn't missed it altogether.

A simple event can avoid the loss of a single input, but what if there is more than one input while the polling loop is unavailable? The most common solution is to create an event queue – that is, a FIFO (first in, first out) queue of events as they occur. The polling loop now reads the event at the front of the queue, processes it and reads the next. It continues like this until the queue is empty, when it simply waits for an event. As long as the queue is big enough, an event queue means you don't miss any input, but input events are not necessarily processed close to the time that they occurred. They should be processed in order, but unless the events are time-stamped the program has no idea when they happened.

An event queue is a common architecture, but to work, or have any advantages, it needs either multiple cores. so that events can always be added to the queue before another occurs, or it needs the help of hardware, usually in the form of interrupts. Notice that an event, or an event queue, cannot increase the program's throughput or its latency, the time to react to an input. In fact, an event queue decreases throughput and increases latency due to overheads of implementation. All an event system does is to ensure that you do not miss any input and that all input gets processed eventually. Interrupts are often confused with events but they are very different. An interrupt is a hardware mechanism that stops the computer doing whatever it is currently doing and makes it transfer its attention to running an interrupt handler. You can think of an interrupt as an event flag that, when set, interrupts the current program to run the assigned interrupt handler. Using interrupts means the outside world decides when the computer should pay attention to input and there is no need for a polling loop. Most hardware people think that interrupts are the solution to everything and polling is inelegant and only to be used when you can't use an interrupt. This is far from the reality.

There is a general feeling that real-time programming and interrupts go together and if you are not using an interrupt you are probably doing something wrong. In fact, the truth is that if you are using an interrupt you are probably doing something wrong. So much so that some organizations are convinced that interrupts are so dangerous that they are banned. Interrupts are only really useful when you have a low-frequency condition that needs to be dealt with on a high-priority basis. Interrupts can simplify the logic of your program, but rarely does using an interrupt speed things up because the overhead involved in interrupt handling is usually quite high. If you have a polling loop that takes 100ms to poll all inputs and there is an input that demands attention in under 60ms then clearly the polling loop is not going to be good enough. Using an interrupt allows the high priority event to interrupt the polling loop and be processed in less than 100ms. However, if this happens very often the polling loop will cease to work as intended. Notice that an alternative is to simply make the polling loop check the input twice per loop.

For a more real-world example, suppose you want to react to a doorbell push button. You could write a polling loop that simply checks the button status repeatedly and forever, or you could write an interrupt service routine (ISR) to respond to the doorbell. The processor would be free to get on with other things until the doorbell was pushed, when it would stop what it was doing and transfer its attention to the ISR. How good a design this is depends on how much the doorbell has to interact with the rest of the program and how many doorbell pushes you are expecting. It takes time to respond to the doorbell push and then the ISR has to run to completion. What is going to happen if another doorbell push happens while the first push is still being processed? Some processors have provision for forming a queue of interrupts, but it doesn't help with the fact that the process can only handle one interrupt at a time. Of course, the same is true of a polling loop, but if you can't handle the throughput of events with a polling loop, you can't handle it using an interrupt either, because interrupts add the time to transfer to the ISR and back again.

Finally, before you dismiss the idea of having a processor do nothing but ask repeatedly "is the doorbell pressed", consider what else it has to do. If the answer is "not much" then a polling loop might well be your simplest option. Also, if the processor has multiple cores, then the fastest way of dealing with any external event is to use one of the cores in a fast polling loop. This can be considered to be a software emulation of a hardware interrupt – not to be confused with a software interrupt or trap, which is a hardware interrupt triggered by software. If you are going to use interrupts to service input then a good design is to use the interrupt handler to feed an event queue. This at least lowers the chance that input will be missed.

Despite their attraction, interrupts are usually a poor choice for anything other than low-frequency events that need to be dealt with quickly.

Asynchronous Buttons

GPIO Zero implements an event-driven approach to asynchronous programming that is presented as if it was an interrupt. You can specify a function to be called when Button is pressed or released using the when_pressed and when_released properties. For example:

```
from gpiozero import Button
from signal import pause
button = Button(4,bounce_time=0.25)

def pressed():
    print("Button pressed")

def released():
    print("Button released")

button.when_pressed =  pressed
button.when_released = released
pause()
```

Notice that you need the pause at the end of the program to stop the program coming to an end. You could just put the program into an infinite loop and do other things while waiting for the button press/release. Also notice that when_pressed and when_released are assigned as references to the functions and the functions are not called until later.

It is important to realize that the `pressed` and `released` functions are called asynchronously – i.e. not synchronized with anything happening in the program. This may be true, but Python only allows one thing to happen at a time and there is no parallelism implied by this form of programming. What happens is that a new thread of execution is started and this simply waits until the event occurs. When the event occurs the event handler is run. When the event handler is run the rest of your program is halted. Python is constructed so as to only allow one part of your Python code to execute at any one time. This is the so-called Global Interpreter Lock or GIL and it means you cannot take advantage of multiple cores to run your Python programs in parallel. Instead the operating system chooses which thread to run at any given time. The thread that is waiting for the event is only started if the event it is waiting for has occurred and then it gets a chance to run the event handler. While the event handler is running you can be sure that no other part of the Python program is running.

You may be attracted by the idea of event handling. It is easy and this makes it great for beginners. Just write what you want to happen when a button is pressed or released and then get on with the rest of your program. No polling loop and no waiting. It is useful for the beginner, but it isn't a good way to organize things in the long run. The problem is that it is the pin factories that are responsible for implementing the event handling and they do this in different ways. As already discussed in connection with general interrupts and events, this approach slows the overall system down and creates problems when events occur at too fast a rate. For example, the pressed event handler can be interrupted by a release event and the release function will run before the press function ends. If a new button press happens after the release, then the press function is run a second time, even if the first call to it is still running. However, the subsequent release function isn't called until the first press function finishes. This is a mess! Exactly what happens when multiple events occur depends on the pin factory that is providing the service and this too is unsatisfactory in that you can't know what will happen.

In conclusion, using event handling in GPIO Zero is an easy way to produce a demo or get started, but it isn't a good way to implement anything beyond the very simple.

This is the big problem with asynchronous code that doesn't use a queue to ensure that multiple events are handled correctly and in the correct order.

If events and asynchronous code aren't the way to do the job what is? The simple answer is the polling loop, but putting order into the polling loop so that it is clean and easy to extend is difficult.

If you are happy with events and basic polling loops skip the next section, which describes a way to organize polling loops so that they are easier to work with.

Finite State Machines

If you are working with an application that requires that you deal with a complex set of input and output lines then you need an organizing principle to save you from the complexity. When you first start writing IoT programs that respond to the outside world, you quickly discover that all of your programs take a similar form:

```
while True:
 wait for some input lines
 process the input data
 write some output lines
 wait for some input lines
 read some more input lines
 write some output lines
```

For most programmers this is a slightly disturbing discovery because programs are not supposed to consist of infinite loops, but IoT programs nearly always, in principle if not in practice, take the form of an infinite polling loop. Another, and more important problem, is that the way in which reading and writing GPIO lines is related can be very complex. So much so that it can be difficult to work out exactly when any particular line is read and when it is written.

We have already seen that events and interrupts are not a good alternative and the polling loop is a really good option, but a simple polling loop needs organization if it is to avoid evolving into something too complex to be understood.

So how should you organize a polling loop so that what it does is self-evident by looking at the code?

There are many answers to this according to the system being implemented, and there are no "pure" theoretical answers that solve all problems, but the finite state machine, FSM, is a model every IoT programmer should know.

A finite state machine is a very simple program. At any given time, the machine (program) has a record of the current state S. At a regular interval, the external world provides an input I which changes the state from S to S' and produces an output O. That's all there is to an FSM. There are variations on the definition, but this one, referred to as a Mealy machine because its outputs depend on both its state and the input, is most suitable for IoT programming.

Your program simply needs to take the form of a polling loop that implements an FSM. It reads the input lines as I and uses this and the current state S to determine the new state S' and the output O. There is some overhead in using this organization, but it is usually worth it. Notice that this organization implies that you read input once, make changes once, and set outputs once in the loop.

FSM Ring Counter

It is difficult to find a good example of using an FSM to control devices because the advantages only really become apparent when things start getting complicated and complication is not the ideal ingredient in an example.

A very common input configuration is the ring counter. A ring counter moves on to a new output each time it receives an input and repeats when it reaches the last output. For example, if you have three output lines connected to three LEDs then initially LED 0 is on, when the user presses the button LED 1 is on and the rest off, the next user-press moves on to LED 2 on and another press turns LED 0 on. You can see that, as the user keeps pressing the button, the LEDs go on and off in a repeating sequence.

A common FSM implementation of a ring counter has a state for each button press and release for each LED being on. For three LEDs this means six states and this has disadvantages. A better idea is to have three states 0, 1 and 2 corresponding to which LED is on. The only complication is that we only want the state to change when the button is pressed, not when it is held or released. The solution to this is to form a "delta", i.e. the change in the measurement from one polling to the next. This is also often thought of and described as an "edge". You can see why if you think of the plot of the level of the GPIO line. When pressed and released the line changes from high to low and there is either a rising or a falling edge in the signal. We are not so much interested in the current level, but the change from high to low, a falling edge, or the change from low to high, a rising edge. In this case we can easily implement software edge detection by taking the difference between readings on two different occasions. A rising edge gives a result of one and a falling edge gives a result of minus one.

In general we want events to be as localized in time as possible and this is the reason that differences in the system are so often used.

Implementing all of this is fairly easy:

```
from gpiozero import Button
from gpiozero import LED
from time import sleep

button = Button(4)
led1=LED(17,initial_value=True)
led2=LED(27)
led3=LED(22)

state=0
buttonState=button.value
while True:
    buttonNow=button.value
    buttonDelta=buttonNow-buttonState
    buttonState=buttonNow
    if state==0:
        if buttonDelta==1:
            state=1
            led1.off()
            led2.on()
            led3.off()

        continue
    if state==1:
        if buttonDelta==1:
            state=2
            led1.off()
            led2.on()
            led3.off()
        continue
    if state==2:
        if buttonDelta==1:
            state=0
            led1.on()
            led2.off()
            led3.off()
        continue
    sleep(0.1)
```

First we set up the LEDs and single Button with led1 on, i.e. we set things up in state 0. Next we start the polling loop which contains an if statement for each of the states. Each if statement tests the buttonDelta, which is only 1 when the button has changed state from released, i.e. 0, to pressed, i.e. 1. If the button is pressed then the state is moved on to the next value, i.e. 0→1, 1→2 and 2→0, and the LEDs are set to the appropriate values. If you try this out you will find that the LEDs do light up sequentially on each button press.

You might think this is more complex than a more "direct" implementation, but it is much easier to extend to more complex situations. Ideally, the names of the states that we use shouldn't refer to inputs or outputs, but to the overall state of the system. For example, if you were using a Pi to control a nuclear reactor you might use a state "CoreMeltdown" in preference to "TempSensorOverLimit". States should be about the consequence of the inputs and the outputs should be the consequence of the current state. In the above example the inputs and output are too simple to give rise to an abstract concept of "state".

Notice that the polling loop is set up so that the whole thing repeats every 100ms. This provides a roughly fixed service time for the sensors. In general, an FSM polling loop takes the following form:

1. An initial reading and processing of the sensors to determine the inputs for this pass through the loop.

2. A set of conditionals which select each possible state.

3. Each state has a set of conditions which change the state and determine the output based on the inputs.

How Fast Can We Measure?

The simplest way to find out how quickly we can take a measurement is to perform a pulse width measurement. By applying in square wave to GPIO4, i.e. pin 7, we can measure the time that the pulse is high using:

```
from gpiozero import Button
from time import perf_counter_ns

button = Button(4)
while True:
        button.wait_for_press()
        button.wait_for_release()
        t1=perf_counter_ns()
        button.wait_for_press()
        t2=perf_counter_ns()
        print((t2-t1)/1000000)
```

This first waits for Button to be pressed, which means the input has gone low. Then we wait for Button to be released, which means the line has gone high, and take the time. Next we wait for the press again which means the line has gone low, again taking the time, and the time difference gives the time the line was high for. If you try this out and feed the input line a square wave from a signal generator, what you will find is that the timings are accurate up to 300Hz on a Pi Zero, 6kHz on a Pi 5 and to 2kHz on a Pi 4. After this they become increasingly unreliable as transitions are missed. Eventually the GPIO Zero implementation of the wait function fails as the state changes while it is being executed.

The `wait_for_` methods aren't very efficient and using a simple read of the button's state is slightly faster:

```
from gpiozero import Button
from time import perf_counter_ns
button = Button(4)
while True:
    while not button.value :pass
    while button.value:pass
    t1 = perf_counter_ns()
    while not button.value :pass
    t2 = perf_counter_ns()
    print((t2-t1)/1000000)
```

Using this method you can obtain speeds as high as 500Hz on a Pi Zero, 9kHz on a Pi 5 and 10kHz on a Pi 4 if you can tolerate the occasional missed pulse.

Notice that in either case, if you try measuring pulse widths much shorter than the lower limit that works, you will get results that look as if longer pulses are being applied. The reason is simply that the Pi will miss the first transition to zero, but will detect a second or third or later transition. This is the digital equivalent of the aliasing effect found in the Fourier Transform or general signal processing.

However you look at it, the maximum input speed of no more than 500Hz is low for any IoT system.

If you don't like the use of `Button` as a general input line, because no button is involved, then, as we aren't using any of the additional `Button` methods, you could create your own custom class or simply use `DigitalInputDevice`:

```
from gpiozero import DigitalInputDevice
from time import perf_counter_ns
pulse = DigitalInputDevice(4)
while True:
    while not pulse.value :pass
    while pulse.value:pass
    t1=perf_counter_ns()
    while not pulse.value :pass
    t2=perf_counter_ns()
    print((t2-t1)/1000000)
```

This works at the same speed as the previous version.

If you want to try using the pin directly, you will see a big speedup:

```
from gpiozero import Device
from time import perf_counter_ns
Device()
pulse = Device.pin_factory.pin(4)
pulse.input_with_pull("up")
while True:
    while not pulse.state :pass
    while pulse.state:pass
    t1=perf_counter_ns()
    while not pulse.state :pass
    t2=perf_counter_ns()
    print((t2-t1)/1000000)
```

This uses the default pin factory, currently `lgpio`. If you try this out you will find that a Pi Zero is reasonable up to 5kHz, a Pi5 works to 100kHz and a Pi4 is reasonably reliable up to 200kHz.

You can see that for input the overhead of running Python is all-important and this is the reason the Pi 4/5 can handle a much faster rate of input. You need to keep in mind that all of these measurements are "best case".

A Custom Simple Input

The `Button` class gives us just about everything we need to implement a simple input device, but occasionally it provides too much and can be misleading. For example, a reed switch really is just a simple switch, but it is controlled by a magnet. Bring a magnet close to a reed switch and it closes, remove the magnet and it opens. There is no sense in which the switch is pressed, released or held in the usual sense – it is just open or closed.

While you can simply use `Button` to work with a reed switch it is worth creating a simple derived class which looks more like a reed switch monitoring a door to its users. In this case the "button" is pressed when the door is closed and released when the door is open:

```
from gpiozero import DigitalInputDevice
class Door(DigitalInputDevice):
    def __init__(self, pin=None, pull_up=True, active_state=None,
                        bounce_time=None,pin_factory=None):
                        super(Door, self).__init__(
            pin, pull_up=pull_up, active_state=active_state,
                bounce_time=bounce_time, pin_factory=pin_factory)
    @property
    def value(self):
        return super(Door, self).value
Door.is_closed = Door.is_active
Door.when_open = Door.when_deactivated
Door.when_closed = Door.when_activated
Door.wait_for_open = Door.wait_for_inactive
Door.wait_for_close = Door.wait_for_active
```

The new `Door` class inherits from `DigitalInputDevice`, which is the class that `Button` inherits from. Its `__init__` function is a modified version of `Button __init__`. The value function returns `0` or `1` according to the door being closed or open respectively. Finally the names of the methods are changed to something that relates to open and closed. You can also remove methods and properties that are no longer appropriate, but in this case they are left for simplicity.

With our new `Door` class we can write things like:

```
door = Door(4)
while True:
    door.wait_for_open()
    print("open")
    door.wait_for_close()
    print("closed")
```

This is no different from using `Button`, but it is easier to understand in the context of a door sensor.

This is so easy to do that there is little reason not to create custom input classes for all simple digital sensors.

Threading

You don't need to know about how this works to use GPIO Zero, so feel free to skip this advanced section and return to it if and when you need it.

Threading isn't normally a topic covered in connection with Python as it is relatively rarely needed. The GPIO Zero library, however, makes a lot of use of threading to allow you to set event handlers that are automatically called when something happens. For example, the `Button` class has a `when_pressed` and a `when_released` attribute that can be assigned to functions that are called when the events occur:

```
def pressed():
    print("Button pressed")

def released():
    print("Button released")

button.when_pressed =  pressed
button.when_released = released
```

Event handling in all of the GPIO Zero library is provided by a mixin – `EventsMixin`. This has `when_activated` and `when_deactivated` properties which are the basis for all event handling in GPIO Zero. This said, not a lot happens regarding events in GPIO Zero. In fact, all that you can do is to store references to functions in the properties and then your program simply carries on running. The actual implementation of the event is done by the pin factories and their pin objects. After all, it is only a pin object that can "know" when something has changed. When a change is detected, the pin factory calls the EventsMixin _fire_events method, which in turn calls the functions that you specified.

The EventsMixin first enters the inheritance hierarchy as part of DigitalInputDevice and SmoothedInputDevice and only classes that inherit from one of these two can handle events. Both classes have when_activated and when_deactivated properties which you use to set the event handling functions.

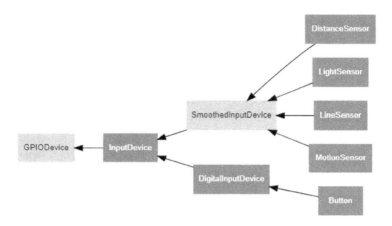

It should be obvious that for an event to happen while your program is running there has to be another thread of execution involved. Each pin factory provides this additional thread in its own way. For example, the NativeFactory has a class called NativeWatchThread that runs on its own thread and waits for a change in a pin's state, either a rising or a falling edge. When this happens the appropriate event handlers are called.

Summary

- There is only one simple input device, `Button`, but it is easy to add custom input devices.

- Exactly how `Button` works depends on how you set the `pull_up` property.

- The simplest way of using `Button` is to `wait_for_press` or `wait_for_release`

- `Button` has a simple debounce feature which sets a "dead" time in which it doesn't respond to any changes.

- Polling is the simplest and fastest way of handling input. It works by repeatedly testing the state of the button.

- The alternative to polling is to use events or interrupts. Both seem to be attractive alternatives, but they have serious difficulties and tend to slow the system down.

- `Button` and other input devices support asynchronous events via the `when_pressed` and `when_released` properties. These can be set to functions which are called when the event occurs.

- Asynchronous events are a very good way to create simple demos and to get started, but they are not efficient and quickly become too complex to understand.

- One way to organize polling so that it remains easy to understand in complex situations, is to use a finite state machine (FSM) approach.

- You can read the state of a button state as quickly as 500Hz on a Pi Zero, 10kHz on a Pi 4 and 9kHz on a Pi 5.

- If you try this out you will find that a Pi Zero is reasonable up to 5kHz, a Pi5 works to 100kHz and a Pi4 is reasonably reliable up to 200kHz

- You can create custom input devices using `DigitalInputDevice` as a base class.

- Python supports threading, which is used to implement GPIO Zero's events.

Chapter 9

Complex Input Devices

The input devices we are about to meet are not complex in the sense of difficult, they just have more features than a simple button. All of the devices inherit from SmoothedInputDevice and the general idea is that a single input isn't sufficient to act on. What is required is an average reading, so reducing noise.

SmoothedInputDevice

The base class for all of this set of input devices is SmoothedInputDevice.

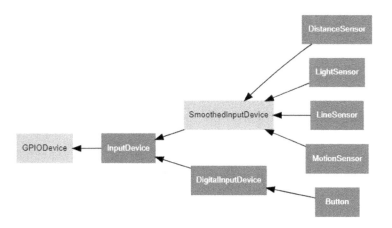

SmoothedInputDevice has all of the properties of InputDevice and, in addition, it sets up a queue of readings. The actual value of the device is obtained by applying a function, usually an average, to the readings in the queue. A background thread is used to take regular readings and the function is computed when you use a value.

The constructor has a large number of parameters:

```
SmoothedInputDevice(pin,pull_up=False, active_state=None,
        threshold=0.5, queue_len=5, sample_wait=0.0,
            partial=False, average=median, ignore=None,
                                        pin_factory=None)
```

The parameters concerned with setting up the queue are:

◆ queue_len
  The length of the queue, i.e. the number of readings that the function is applied to. The default is 5.

◆ threshold
  The value that is used as a cut-off for the device being activated. If the read value is greater than threshold, the device is active.

◆ sample_wait
  The time between readings in seconds. The default is 0, which means read as fast as possible.

◆ partial
  If True an attempt to read the device returns with a value, even if the queue isn't full. If False, the default, a read blocks until the queue is full.

◆ ignore
  A set of values that represents non-readings and should be ignored in the calculation of the average. Defaults to None.

◆ average
  The function applied to the values in the queue to get the final value. It defaults to median, which is the middle value in the queue.

Using a SmoothedInputDevice is just a matter of setting up the degree of smoothing needed – i.e. the speed of reading, the number of data points to average, and the function that should be used to average them.

It should be obvious that, whatever the SmoothInputDevice is reading, it can't be a single GPIO line that returns a 0 or a 1. In most cases averaging this using median would return 0.5. However, averaging using average would give you a value that was proportional to the ratio of ones to zeros in the measurement interval. In the same way, you can create a device which returns a number proportional to the time a GPIO line is high.

Using the TRCT5000 Line Sensor

The LineSensor device makes use of a module based on the TRCT5000 infrared emitter and sensor.

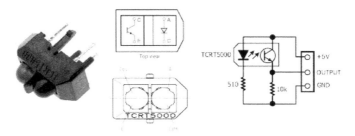

To make this suitable for use with a GPIO line you need to add some electronics:

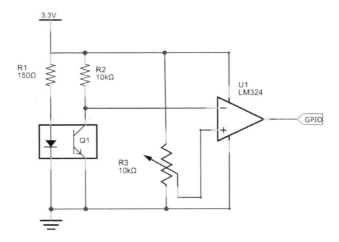

The IR diode sends a beam of IR out of the device and if it is reflected back, the photo transistor switches on. The LM324 U1 outputs a high signal when the voltage from the IR sensor is greater than that set on the potentiometer, R3. That is, R3 acts as a sensitivity control.

You don't need to build the circuit because you can buy ready-built modules:

You simply connect the three pins to 3.3V, ground and a GPIO line of your choice. It is worth knowing that some modules output high when over a white line and some go low.

Once you have the hardware connected you can create a LineSensor using the constructor:

```
LineSensor(pin, queue_len=5, sample_rate=100, threshold=0.5,
                                partial=False, pin_factory=None)
```

You can read the value property to discover if the sensor is over a reflective surface or not:

```
from gpiozero import LineSensor
sensor = LineSensor(4)
while True:
    if sensor.value>0.5:
        print('Line detected')
    else:
        print('No line detected')
```

You can also use the wait_for_line, wait_for_no_line, when_line and when_no_line events.

In practice, setting the threshold control on the hardware is likely to be more important than tuning the software.

D-SUN PIR Motion Sensor

Infrared motion detectors work by sensing a change in the level of infrared radiation. The D-SUN PIR is a standard low-cost module, but you can use any that follow the basic design with a three-pin connection – Vcc, Ground and Data. The data line is set high when motion is detected. Different devices have different controls for sensitivity and usually a setting for repeatable or non-repeatable mode. In repeatable mode the output goes high when motion is detected and the device is reset after a set time so that it is ready to detect motion again. In non-repeatable mode the output is set high as long as motion is detected.

To use the device all you have to do is connect the Vcc pin to 5V, the ground pin to ground and the data pin to the GPIO line you want to use.

You can create a `MotionSensor` object using the constructor:

```
MotionSensor(pin,queue_len=1, sample_rate=10, threshold=0.5,
                                partial=False, pin_factory=None)
```

Notice that the default for `queue_len` is 1, meaning that no smoothing is performed. To discover if motion has been detected you can use `value` or `motion_detected` which compares `value` to the `threshold`. You can also use the `wait_for_motion`, `wait_for_no_motion`, `when_motion` and `when_no_motion` events.

Light Sensor

There are many different types of light sensor, but the LDR, Light Dependent Resistor, is one of the simplest.

As its name suggests, it simply changes its resistance according to how much light falls on it. Using it to sense the light level is simply a matter of measuring its resistance. This can be done directly, and you can also use the resistance to change other physical properties of a system. For example, you can charge a capacitor to a set voltage and then time how long it takes to discharge through the resistor. This is how the LightSensor class works.

You need to set up the simple circuit shown below. What happens is that,

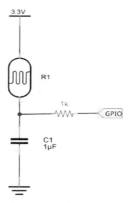

when a reading is required, the GPIO line is set to low, which discharges the capacitor. Then it is set to input, which allows the capacitor to charge through the LDR. The GPIO line reads 0 until the capacitor has charged enough to make it read 1. The time to read 1 is proportional to the resistance, which in turn is proportional to the light falling on it.

The only problem we have is that different LDRs have different resistances and hence different charge times. You can work out the charge times, but the simplest thing to do is to adjust the time by trial and error.

you have the circuit connected to the GPIO line of your choice, you can create a `LightSensor` object using the constructor:

```
LightSensor(pin, queue_len=5, charge_time_limit=0.01,
            threshold=0.1, partial=False, pin_factory=None)
```

The new element here is the `charge_time_limit` which is the time in seconds it takes the capacitor to charge enough to change the zero input to a one. The default should be close to the value you need, but you might have to tune it by trial and error to the range of light inputs that you want to work with, i.e. what you consider light and what you consider dark. Also notice that by default five readings are taken. An LDR changes its resistance slowly in response to a sudden light change. You can use the `light_detected` property to see if the light exceeds the threshold or the `value` property to measure the light level. You can also use the `wait_for_dark`, `wait_for_light`, `when_dark` and `when_light` events.

A Custom Complex Input Device

The `LightSensor` class is more useful than it appears. As it detects the time it takes for a capacitor to discharge, it can be used to measure resistance or capacitance. If the resistor is fixed then the time depends on the value of the capacitor. If the capacitor is fixed then the time depends on the value of the resistor. Any sensor that varies its resistance or capacitance in response to external conditions can be used with the `LightSensor` class. For example, a thermistor is a temperature-dependent resistor and can be read using the `LightSensor` class.

You can create a presence sensor by using a metal plate as one side of a capacitor. As people move closer or further away its capacitance changes and hence you can use it with the `LightSensor` class. This is the principle behind many touch sensitive switches.

As an example, we can create a simple moisture sensor. You need to construct two metal probes that can be stuck into the soil. The probes have to be non-corrosive and we used a pair of metal kebab skewers held in place by being passed through a plastic wire connector block, which also makes the task of connecting to the skewers easy. The block also holds the skewers apart at a fixed distance and makes putting them into the soil easier. Of course, the accuracy of measurement depends on the contact with the soil and minimization of movement.

The circuit is exactly the same as for the LightSensor, but with the resistor replaced by the moisture sensor:

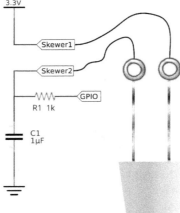

As there is no difference between this and the LightSensor, you could just use the LightSensor class to implement the moisture sensor. However, it is easy to modify the name of LightSensor and change some of its methods:

```
from gpiozero import LightSensor

class Moisture(LightSensor):
    def __init__(self, pin=None, queue_len=5,
                 charge_time_limit=0.01, threshold=0.1,
                 partial=False, pin_factory=None):
        super(Moisture, self).__init__(pin, threshold=threshold,
            queue_len=queue_len,charge_time_limit=charge_time_limit,
```

```
pin_factory=pin_factory)
Moisture.wait_for_dry=Moisture.wait_for_light
Moisture.wait_for_wet=Moisture.wait_for_dark
Moisture.when_dry=Moisture.when_light
Moisture.when_wet=Moisture.when_dark
```

The only real difference is that now the resistance of the soil can be in the range 100Ω to 500KΩ, or even higher, depending on soil structure and the amount of contact and distance between the probes. You can adjust for this by changing the size of the capacitor or you can modify charge_time_limit, for example:

```
moisture = Moisture(4,charge_time_limit = 0.5,threshold = 0.6)
for d in moisture.values:
    print(d)
```

You have to find the appropriate values of both parameters by experiment.

If you have a raw sensor that works in terms of resistance or capacitance then the same procedure will produce a suitable class to work with it.

HC-SR04 Distance Sensor

An ultrasonic distance sensor works by sending out a pulse of ultrasonic sound and timing how long it takes to detect an echo. There are a number of similar modules on the market, but the HC-SR04 is common and inexpensive.

However, it needs to work with 5V data lines and this means using a divider to shift the voltage to 3.3V. A simpler solution is to use the HC-SR04P, which is nearly as cheap and works at 3.3V.

Whichever module you use, there are four connections V_{cc}, Ground, Trig (Trigger) and Echo. You have to connect each of Trig and Echo to a GPIO line. The basic operation is that the Trig line is set high for a short time and this causes the module to send a pulse. The Echo line goes high when a reflected pulse is detected. The time between the two events gives you the distance.

The constructor requires that you specify the two pins used as the first two parameters:

```
DistanceSensor(echo, trigger, queue_len=30, max_distance=1,
        threshold_distance=0.3, partial=False, pin_factory=None)
```

Notice that readings are the smoothed average of 30 measurements – ultrasonic distance measuring is very noisy. You can also specify a `max_distance` which is use to scale the `value` parameter. The `threshold_distance` is used to specify a "too close" event via

- ◆ `wait_for_in_range`
- ◆ `wait_for_out_of_range,`
- ◆ `when_in_range`
- ◆ `when_out_of_range.`

The `distance` property gives an estimate of the current distance from 0 to `max_distance` and `value` gives a scaled distance in the range 0 to 1.

Source/Values – An Alternative Approach

We have already seen that events are a good way of getting things done simply when it comes to input. They might not scale well to more serious applications, but they make simple programs even simpler. GPIO Zero also offers a way to "connect" input and output devices. This is sophisticated in its implementation, but, as with events, it is very easy to use – at least initially. You don't need to know about, or make use of, the source/values approach to programming devices, but it provides another approach to the problem of creating a program – declarative programming. This is where, instead of writing instructions that tell the machine what to do at every step, you simply write something that specifies what you want.

Every GPIO Zero device has a value property, which indicates its current state as a zero or one. Input devices have a read-only value property, they are sources of data, and output devices have a read/write value property that can be regarded as a data sink. You can connect together a data input with a data output using the source property. For example:

```
led.source=button
```

connects the button's value to the LED's value such that any changes in the button's value is communicated to the LED. It is as if you were running:

```
while True:
    led.value=button.value
```

which is more or less what actually happens, but as the code is being run in a background thread, your program can get on and do something else. The result is that you have "wired up" the button to the LED in software and now, every time you press the button, the LED will light up and every time you release it, the LED will switch off.

Values are updated once every hundredth of a second, so the background program is:

```
while True:
    led.value=button.value
    sleep(0.01)
```

You can change the rate of update by setting the source_delay property to the time between values. For example:

```
led.source.source_delay=0.5
```

sets the update to once every half a second. You can set the update rate for each device via its source_delay property.

Every device also has a `values` property which converts its `value` property into an iterator. For example, to repeatedly print the `value` property of the button, you can write:

```
for d in button.values:
    print(d)
```

The `values` property is used by the `source` property to retrieve values. You don't need to know how the `values` property is created to use it, but isn't complicated:

```
@property
def values(self):
    while True:
        try:
            yield self.value
        except DeviceClosed:
            break
```

You can see that reading `values` creates an infinite loop that keeps returning the `value` property until something goes wrong. This is used to connect two devices together.

You can take this "wiring" a stage further and make chains of connected `value` properties. For example:

```
led1.source=button
led2.source=led1
```

would result in both LEDs turning on when the button was pressed.

You can also go beyond zero and one. Some input devices return a value between 0 and 1 and some return values outside of this range. As long as the input value range and the output value range are similar, you can connect them together. For example, the light or the distance sensor described earlier outputs a value in the range 0 to 1. There is also a `PWMLED`, which we will meet in detail in the next chapter, which has a value that can be set between 0 and 1 to set its brightness level. We can connect any of these together. For example:

```
from gpiozero import PWMLED, DistanceSensor
from signal import pause

led=PWMLED(4)
dist=DistanceSensor(5,6)
led.source=dist
pause
```

results in an LED that gets brighter as something moves away from the distance sensor.

What if you wanted the LED to get brighter as something approached?

The answer is you can put other objects in the chain of values that can process the data. GPIO Zero provides some standard value processing functions including the following source functions.

- `absoluted(values)`
  Takes the absolute value of each value.

- `booleanized(values,min,max,hysteresis=0)`
  `True` for values in the range `min` to `max` and `False` otherwise. The `hysteresis` parameter sets the amount of change that is allowed without changing the state. That is, if the value is greater than `max` then the cutoff is `max-hysteresis` and if it is smaller than `max` has to increase to `max` plus `hysteresis` before the state is changed.

- `clamped(value,output_min=0,output_max=1)`
  Truncates values to be in the range `output_min` to `output_max`.

- `inverted(values,input_min=0,input_max=1)`
  Inverts the value using `input_max` minus value plus `input_mi`

- `negated(values)`
  Swaps `True` and `False`.

- `post_delayed(values,delay)`
  Waits for `delay` seconds after returning the value.

- `pre_delayed(values,delay)`
  Waits for `delay` seconds before returning value

- `scaled(values,output_min,output_max,input_min=0,input_max=1)`
  Re-scales the values using value*(output_max-output_min) divided by(input_max-input_min) plus output_min

- `post_periodic_filtered(values, repeat_after, block)`
  After `repeat_after` items, blocks the next `block` items from `values`. So `post_periodic_filtered(values, 1,1)` discards even items.

- `pre_periodic_filtered(values, block, repeat_after)`
  Blocks the next `block` of items from `values` and after `repeat_after` items repeats the block. So `pre_periodic_filtered(values, 100,0)` discards the first 100 values and `pre_periodic_filtered(values, 1,1)` discards all odd values.

- `quantized(values, steps, input_min=0, input_max=1)`
  Converts to discrete values between `input_min` and `input_max` using `int(value*steps)/steps*(input_max-input_min)+input_min`

- `queued(values, qsize)`
  Forms a queue of `qsize` values and only passes them on when the queue is full.

- `smoothed(values, qsize, function)`
  Forms a queue of `qsize` value and then applies the function specified by *function*, by default `average`, to them, so reducing them to a single value.

To return to the problem of making the LED glow brighter as something moves closer, you can see that all we need to do is use the inverted function to turn 0 to 1 into 1 to 0:

```
from gpiozero import PWMLED, DistanceSensor
from gpiozero.tools import inverted
from signal import pause
led=PWMLED(4)
dist=DistanceSensor(5,6)
led.source=inverted(dist)
pause
```

We don't need to specify the input_max and input_min parameters because they default to 1 and 0.

As well as functions which can transform the values there are also functions which can combine values from multiple sources. Each of these functions accepts any number of parameters:

- all_values(*values)
  Returns True if all of the values are True.

- any_values(*values)
  Returns True if any of the values is True.

- averaged(*values)
  Returns the average of all the values.

- multiplied(*values)
  Returns the product of all the values.

- summed(*values)
  Returns the sum of all the values.

- zip_values(*values)
  Returns a tuple of all the values.

For example, if you have distance sensors on the back and front of a robot you can set an LED to the average distance using:

```
from gpiozero import PWMLED, DistanceSensor
from gpiozero.tools import inverted,averaged
from signal import pause

led=PWMLED(4)
front=DistanceSensor(5,6)
back=DistanceSensor(7,8)
led.source=averaged(front,back)
pause
```

A Custom Combining Function

Even though there are so many combining functions, there is usually a need for something specialized. For example, what about a function that returns the minimum value? If you take a look at the source code for any of the functions listed above, you should have no difficulty in seeing how to create your own. In this case, our custom mined function is:

```
from gpiozero.tools import _normalize
def mined(*values):
    values = [_normalize(v) for v in values]
    for v in zip(*values):
        yield min(v)
```

If you are sure that the values are all in standard form, i.e. created by devices or functions in GPIO Zero, you can omit the call to _normalize. The core of the function simply uses zip to create a tuple of all of the readings and then applies the standard Python min function to each tuple, yielding on the result.

You can replace the min function by max or whatever you need to create your own transformation of the data.

Once you have the mined function you can create a program that lights the LED according to the closest approach from the back or the front:

```
from gpiozero import PWMLED, DistanceSensor
from gpiozero.tools import _normalize

def mined(*values):
    values = [_normalize(v) for v in values]
    for v in zip(*values):
        yield min(v)
from signal import pause

led=PWMLED(4)
front=DistanceSensor(5,6)
back=DistanceSensor(7,8)
led.source=mined(front,back)
pause
```

Now the LED is set to the smallest of the readings from the front and back distance sensors.

As well as devices providing streams of data, there are also functions which generate values that can be fed to output devices or other functions as data sources:

- ◆ `alternating_values(initial_value=False)`
  Alternates between True and False.

- ◆ `cos_values(period=360) sin_values(period=360)`
  A cosine or sine wave which repeats after period values. As the background update occurs once every hundredth of a second setting period to 100 gives a 1Hz waveform. Notice that the values are between -1 and 1 and if you want a different range you need to use scaled.

- ◆ `ramping_values(period=360)`
  A triangle wave which increases from 0 to 1 and back again every period values.

- ◆ `random_values()`
  Random values between 0 and 1.

The simplest example of using these functions is to make an LED twinkle:

```
from gpiozero import PWMLED
from gpiozero.tools import random_values
from signal import pause
led = PWMLED(4)
led.source = random_values()
pause()
```

It is relatively easy to create a custom value source. For example, to control PWM, Pulse Width Modulation, which is explored in the next chapter, you can produce a cycle of values with `period*duty` set to 1 and the remainder set to 0. For example:

```
PWM_values(10,0.5)
```

repeatedly produces five values of 1 and five of 0.

The function is:

```
def PWM_values(period=360,duty=0.5):
    _ontime=int(period*duty)
    _offtime=period-_ontime
    data=[1]*_ontime+[0]*_offtime
    while True:
        for i in range(_ontime):
            print(1)
            yield 1
        for i in range(_offtime):
            print(0)
            yield 0
```

It is very simple, consisting of two for loops that produce _ontime ones and _offtime zeros over and over again.

You can use the same technique to develop your own function. Usually it is better first to write a function that produces the sequence of values that you want and after you have verified that this works convert it into a generator by adding `yield`.

Internal Devices

GPIO Zero supports a number of devices that are either built into the Pi or derive from information that the Pi can supply. These are often useful in source/value chains. The internal device functions have changed to support events in GPIO Zero 2. They all work in the same basic way in that they return an object that you can use to find the internal device's value, call an event handling routine or use in a source/value chain. There is usually a max and min parameter that sets the range that the value property will be set to 1. How they work becomes clear when you have seen one of the functions in detail:

◆ `TimeOfDay(start_time, end_time, utc=True, event_delay=5.0 pin_factory=None)`

where `utc=`True uses UTC instead of local time and `event_delay` is the time between updates.

Returns a `TimeOfDay` object with the following properties:

end_time	same as end_time parameter
start_time	same as start_time parameter
utc	same as utc parameter
is_active	True if time is between start_time and end_time
value	returns 1 when time is between start_time and end_time
when_activated	function to run when status changes to active
when_deactivated	function to run when status changes to deactive

You can use `TimeOfDay` either by setting functions that are called when the start_time or end_time is reached or you can use value as a data source. The example in the documentation connects an LED to the value so as to switch it on for the time interval. Notice that you don't need a time property to return the current time as this is available from the standard Python function `time`.

Once you have seen `TimeOfDay` the other internal functions are obvious:

- `PingServer(host, event_delay=10, pin_factory=None)`

  Pings the URL or IP address of the server and returns a `PingServer` object. Activation is defined by the host responding and `value` is 1 if it has returned even a single ping.

- ```
  CPUTemperature(
    sensor_file='/sys/class/thermal/thermal_zone0/temp',
    min_temp=0.0, max_temp=100.0,
    threshold=80.0, event_delay=5, pin_factory=None)
  ```

  Checks the CPU temperature using the default sensor file.
  The `min_temp` and `max_temp` set the temperatures for which a 0 and a 1 are returned by `value`:

  `value=(temperature-min_temp)/(max_temp-min_temp)`

  and `threshold` sets the critical temperature above which the device is active. You can use the `temperature` property to read the temperature.

- ```
  LoadAverage(load_average_file='/proc/loadavg',
    min_load_average=0.0, max_load_average=1.0,
    threshold=0.8, minutes=5,event_delay=5, pin_factory=None)
  ```

  Gets the average CPU load from the default file.
  The `min_load_average` and `max_load_average` set the loads that corresponds to:

  ```
  value=(load_average-min_load_average)/
              (max_load_average-min_load_average)
  ```

  a value between 0 and 1 when `load_average` is between `max_load_average` and `min_load_average` .

  `Threshold` sets the device to active if the load exceeds the `value`. The `minutes` parameter gives the time over which the load is averaged. The `load_average` property can be used to find the current value.

- ```
  DiskUsage(filesystem='/',threshold=90.0,event_delay=30,
                                  pin_factory=None)
  ```

  Checks the amount of disk space used by the folder specified by filesystem and all its sub-folders. If the amount is greater than the `threshold` percentage the device is set to active. The `usage` property returns the current percentage use and `value` is `usage/100`.
  ```

For example, to turn an LED on when the temperature is too high:

```
from gpiozero import LED, CPUTemperature
from signal import pause
from gpiozero.tools import booleanized

cpu = CPUTemperature(min_temp=58, max_temp=90)
print(cpu.temperature)
led=LED(4)
led.source = booleanized(cpu,0,1)
pause()
```

We need to use the booleanized function to convert the decimal value to an on/off or 0 1 value that can be used by the LED.

A Custom Internal Device

It is easy to add a custom internal device. As an example, let's create a new class that returns the fraction of free memory. The /proc/meminfo file gives memory use statistics. You can open it and read it or just use the cat command:

```
cat /proc/meminfo
MemTotal:         949444 kB
MemFree:          250276 kB
MemAvailable:     588716 kB
Buffers:           94528 kB
Cached:           355420 kB
SwapCached:            0 kB
Active:           454272 kB
Inactive:         193148 kB
```

So to get the free memory we have to read the file and extract the value in the second line. The new class is:

```
import io
from gpiozero import InternalDevice

class MemoryFree(InternalDevice):
    def __init__(self, threshold=0.9, memfile='/proc/meminfo',
                                       pin_factory=None):
        super(MemoryFree, self).__init__(pin_factory=pin_factory)
        self._fire_events(self.pin_factory.ticks(), None)
        self.memfile = memfile
        self.threshold = threshold
        self._totalmem = 0
        self._availablemem = 0
```

```python
    @property
    def free_mem(self):
        with io.open(self.memfile, 'r') as f:
            self._totalmem = int(f.readline().strip().split()[1])
            freemem = int(f.readline().strip().split()[1])
            self._availablemem =
                        int(f.readline().strip().split()[1])
            return freemem

    @property
    def value(self):
        return self.free_mem/self._availablemem

    @property
    def is_active(self):
        return self.value < 1-self.threshold
```

The constructor lets you specify a threshold for memory used rather than free so that the device is active if used memory goes above the threshold – this can be easily changed. The freemem property opens the file, reads the first three lines and extracts the total memory, free memory and available memory. The free memory is returned as the result. The value property returns a value between 0 and 1 indicating the percentage of free memory and the is_active property is True if memory use exceeds the threshold. Notice that the call to fire_events is included just in case event support is added to the base class.

Using this new class we can light an LED according to how much free memory there is:

```python
from gpiozero import PWMLED
from signal import pause

led = PWMLED(4)

mem = MemoryFree(0.1)
print(mem.value, flush=True)
print(mem.is_active, flush=True)


led.source=mem
pause()
```

You can use similar code to add any internal or non-GPIO based devices to GPIO Zero.

The Limitations of Source/Values?

The idea of using declarative programming is a good one and there is no quicker way of implementing a demonstration program to connect a Button to an LED, say. In this respect using Source/Values is a good way to introduce the basic ideas, but it soon becomes clear that things get complicated once you move beyond simple demonstrations. This sort of declarative programming rapidly becomes difficult to understand as different devices affect each other in ways that can be difficult to deduce from the program. What is more, the order in which things happen is completely arbitrary and the approach is so inefficient that you can only hope to do things that don't need fast processing. You could say that the Source/Value approach has all of the disadvantages of events and interrupts, but even more so. This approach to the IoT and physical computing is good to know about, but it is not ideal for real-world applications.

Summary

- `SmoothedInputDevice` is the base class for a set of more sophisticated input devices which average or process their raw inputs in some way.

- The `LineSensor` class uses a IR diode and sensor to detect the reflectivity of a surface.

- `MotionSensor` is a standard IR motion sensor.

- `LightSensor` uses an LDR to measure the current light level. It can be used to measure resistance or capacitance. For example, you can use it to measure the moisture content of soil.

- `DistanceSensor` is a standard ultrasonic distance sensor.

- The Source/Values mechanism can be use to connect output devices to input devices so that the input is transferred to the output every hundredth of a second.

- To make Source/Values more useful, there are functions that can transform and combine values.

- There are also functions that can generate values to be fed to output devices and it is easy to create your own.

- A number of internal devices can also act as sources of values.

Chapter 10
Pulse Width Modulation

One way around the problem of getting a fast response from a microcontroller is to move the problem away from the processor. In the case of the Pi's processor there are some built-in devices that can use GPIO lines to implement protocols without the CPU being involved. In this chapter we take a close look at pulse width modulation (PWM) including generating sound and driving LEDs.

When performing their most basic function, i.e. output, the GPIO lines can be set high or low by the processor. How quickly they can be set high or low depends on the speed of the processor.

Using the GPIO line in its Pulse Width Modulation (PWM) mode you can generate pulse trains up to 4.8MHz, i.e. pulses just a little more than $0.08\mu s$. The reason for the increase in speed, a factor of at least 100, is that the GPIO is connected to a pulse generator and, once set to generate pulses of a specific type, the pulse generator just gets on with it without needing any intervention from the GPIO line or the processor. In fact, the pulse output can continue after your program has ended if you forget to reset it.

Of course, even though the PWM line can generate pulses as short as $0.1\mu s$, it can only change the pulses it produces each time that the processor can modify them. For example, you can't use PWM to produce a single $0.1\mu s$ pulse because you can't disable the PWM generator in just $0.1\mu s$.

Hardware-generated PWM sounds like a really good idea, and it is, but there is a problem. At the time of writing, none of the pin factories actually support the use of hardware for PWM. They all generate PWM signals using software although two pin factories, `rpio` and `pigpio`, use advanced methods that put minimum load on the CPU.

At the moment the default pin factory, `lgpio`, supports only software-implemented PWM. While this means you can use any pin as a PWM output, the speed is limited by how much power the CPU can dedicate to the task.

The alternatives offer some advantages and some big disadvantages as discussed in Chapter 6. `pigpio` uses DMA to generate PWM signals, but by making use of a daemon – a driver that runs all the time in the background. There are suggestions that this daemon isn't 100% stable, it doesn't support Pi 5 and support for Pi 4 is still experimental. However, the project does seem alive and well.

I would advise using `rpigpio`, the previous default pin factory if you can and if you really need high-speed PWM then I would suggest moving to C and working with the hardware directly. Here we will mostly ignore the hardware PWM features of the Pi. If you want to make use of them, see *Raspberry Pi IoT in C, 3rd Ed*: ISBN:9781871962840.

Some Basic Pi PWM Facts

There are some facts worth getting clear right from the start, although their full significance will only become clear as we progress.

First what is PWM? The simple answer is that a Pulse Width Modulated signal has pulses that repeat at a fixed rate, say, one pulse every millisecond, but the width of the pulse can be changed. There are two basic things to specify about the pulse train that is generated, its repetition rate and the width of each pulse. Usually the repetition rate is set as a simple repeat period and the width of each pulse is specified as a percentage of the repeat period, referred to as the duty cycle.

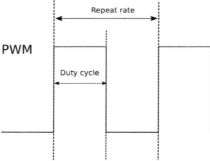

So, for example, a 1ms repeat and a 50% duty cycle specifies a 1ms period, which is high for 50% of the time, i.e. a pulse width of 0.5ms.

The two extremes are 100% duty cycle, i.e. the line is always high, and 0% duty cycle, i.e. the line is always low. The duty cycle is simply the proportion of time the line is set high. Notice it is the duty cycle that carries the information in PWM and not the frequency. What this means is that, generally, you select a repeat rate and stick to it and what you change as the program runs is the duty cycle.

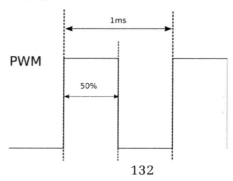

In many cases PWM is implemented using special PWM-generating hardware that is either built into the processor chip or provided by an external chip. The processor simply sets the repeat rate by writing to a register and then changing the duty cycle by writing to another register. This generally provides the best sort of PWM with no load on the processor and, generally, glitch-free operation. You can even buy add-on boards that will provide additional channels of PWM without adding to the load on the processor.

The alternative to dedicated PWM hardware is to implement it in software. You can quite easily work out how to do this. All you need is to set a timing loop to set the line high at the repetition rate and then set it low again according to the duty cycle. You can implement this either using interrupts or a polling loop and in more advanced ways, such as using a DMA (Direct Memory Access) channel.

In the case of the Pi, the PWM lines are implemented using special PWM hardware but, as already mentioned, at the time of writing, none of the pin factories supports using hardware PWM. The standard RPi.GPIO factory supports software-implemented PWM on any GPIO pin and this is the factory used in the rest of this chapter.

As you can guess, there are no PWM inputs, just output. If for some reason you need to decode, or respond to, a PWM input then you need to program it using the GPIO input lines and the pulse measuring techniques introduced in previous chapters.

Using PWM

The direct way of using PWM is to create an instance of the PWMOutputDevice class, yet this is listed as a base class as if it wasn't to be used in everyday programming. This couldn't be further from the truth and, if you hope to do anything even slightly innovative you need to know about PWMOutputDevice. There is no real excuse as it is very easy to use.

If you create an instance, using GPIO4 say:

```
pwm=PWMOutputDevice(4)
```

then there are just two important properties, frequency and value. The frequency property sets the PWM repeat rate and value sets the duty cycle as a fraction. For example:

```
pwm.frequency=1000
pwm.value=0.5
```

sets a frequency of 1kHz and a duty cycle of 0.5, i.e. 50%.

Putting this together gives:

```
from gpiozero import PWMOutputDevice
from signal import pause
pwm=PWMOutputDevice(4)
pwm.frequency=10000
pwm.value=0.5
pause()
```

Notice that you have to use pause to keep the program running as the PWM isn't hardware-generated. The program has to be "doing something", even if it is only sleeping so that it can update the PWM state.

If you are using rpigpio and look at the signal using a logic analyzer you will be dismayed to discover that it isn't a 1kHz signal:

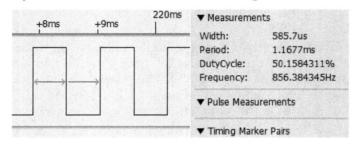

As in most cases the duty cycle is what is important, not the frequency, an inaccuracy of 150Hz may not matter. For the Pi Zero you need to specify a frequency roughly 20% greater than you need. For example, a frequency of 1200Hz gives a PWM signal of 1000Hz within a few Hertz.

A plot of specified frequency versus actual for the Pi Zero reveals that 6kHz is as fast as you can go:

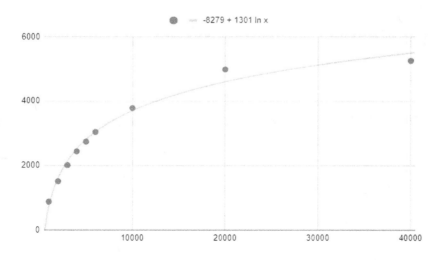

134

The plot for the Pi 4 is very similar:

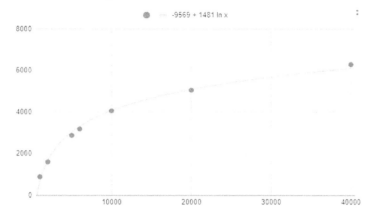

The LGPIOFactory, which is the only one that works on the Pi 5 is limited to 10kHz and is relatively accurate over this range.

Comparing this performance to hardware-generated PWM, it is slow. However, for many applications this doesn't matter. For example, to use PWM to control a servo you only need a frequency of 50Hz.

The problem with the frequency error also occurs in the setting of the duty cycle. The software detects duty cycles of 0 and 1 and correctly sets the line low or high respectively. However, for values close to 0 or 1 you get a duty cycle longer or shorter than requested.

The results for a Pi 4 and Pi Zero using `rpigpio` are very similar:

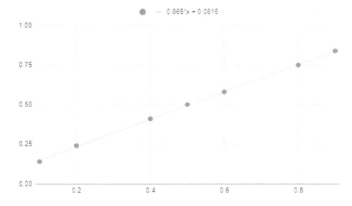

Note: x axis is set to the duty cycle and y is measured

Notice that there is a sudden jump to duty cycles of 0 and 1 which isn't shown in the graph.

If you use the latest default pin factory, `lgpio`, then you will find that it too has trouble with small and very large values of duty cycle:

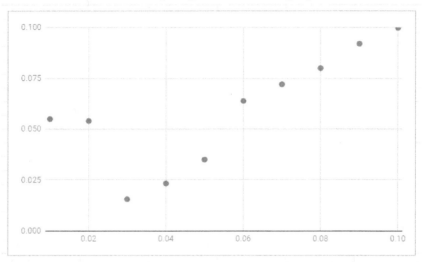

Note: x axis is set to the duty cycle and y is measured

How Fast Can You Modulate?

For reasons that will be discussed later, in most cases, the whole point is to vary the duty cycle, or the period of the pulse train. This means that the next question is how fast can you change the characteristic of a PWM line? In other words, how fast can you change the duty cycle? There is no easy way to give an exact answer and, in most applications, an exact answer isn't of much use. The reason is that for a PWM signal to convey information it generally has to deliver a number of complete cycles with a given duty cycle. This is because of the way pulses are often averaged in applications.

We also have another problem – synchronization. There is no way to swap from one duty cycle to another exactly when a complete duty cycle has just finished. All you can do is use a timer to estimate when the pulse is high or low. What this means is that there is going to be a glitch when you switch from one duty cycle to another. Of course, this glitch becomes less important as you slow the rate of duty cycle change and exactly what is usable depends on the application. To illustrate the problem consider the following program:

```
from gpiozero import PWMOutputDevice
pwm=PWMOutputDevice(4)
pwm.frequency=1000
while True:
    pwm.value=0.1
    pwm.value=0.9
```

136

It generates a 1kHz PWM signal and attempts to change from 10% to 90% duty cycle as fast as possible. The result is that the number of pulses you get for each duty cycle is very variable:

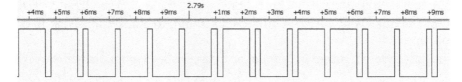

The conclusion is that, using software-generated PWM, there is no easy way to create an accurate waveform that changes its duty cycle in a controllable way unless the change is very slow.

More PWM Methods

Really, all you need to use PWM is a way to set the frequency and the duty cycle, but the PWMOutputDevice has a few more methods which you might want to use.

The on and off methods set the line high and low and stop all PWM output. Setting a frequency or a duty cycle starts the output again.

The toggle method is slightly odd in that it changes the output from a duty cycle of D to a duty cycle of 1-D. So, for example:

```
from gpiozero import PWMOutputDevice
from time import sleep
pwm=PWMOutputDevice(4)
pwm.frequency=1000
pwm.value=0.1
while True:
    sleep(0.5)
    pwm.toggle()
```

produces a signal that has a duty cycle of 10% for half a second and then 90% for the next half a second and so on.

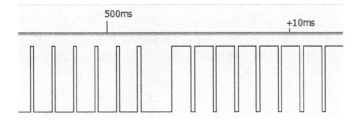

The `pulse` method may seem strange, but it makes more sense after we have looked at how a PWM signal is used to control the flow of power to a device, an LED in particular.

```
pulse(fade_in_time=1, fade_out_time=1, n=None, background=True)
```

What `pulse` does is to vary the duty cycle from 0 to 1 and then back to 0 again. For example:

```
pwm.pulse(fade_in_time=0.5,fade_out_time=1,n=3,background=False)
```

starts with a duty cycle of 0 and slowly increases it to 1 over half a second and then decreases it from 1 to 0 in 1 second. The n=3 means that it repeats this three times. If you set the duty cycle to 0, or just leave it out, the pulsing continues forever. The `background=False` makes Python wait for the number of pulses to complete. If you set it to `True` then your program carries on at once and the pulsing happens in the background.

The `blink` method is very similar to `pulse` but you can specify a full on and full off time. That is, the PWM signal starts from a 0% duty cycle, fades in up to 100%, stays at 100% for the `on_time` and then fades out to 0% duty cycle and stays off for the specified `off_time`.

```
blink(on_time=1, off_time=1, fade_in_time=0, fade_out_time=0,
                                    n=None, background=True)
```

Controlling an LED

What sorts of things do you use PWM for?

There are lots of very clever uses for PWM. However, there are two use cases which account for most PWM applications - voltage or power modulation and signaling to servos. We will look at servos and motors in the next chapter. As a first practical example, let's control the brightness of an LED.

The amount of power delivered to a device by a pulse train is proportional to the duty cycle. A pulse train that has a 50% duty cycle is delivering current to the load only 50% of the time and this is irrespective of the pulse repetition rate. So the duty cycle controls the power, but the period still matters in many situations because you want to avoid any flashing or other effects. A higher frequency smooths out the power flow at any duty cycle.

Notice that, as the LED when powered by a PWM signal is either full on or full off, there is no effect of the change in LED light output with current, the LED is always run at the same current.

For a simple example we need to connect a standard LED to the PWM line and can use the BJT driver circuit introduced in Chapter 7.

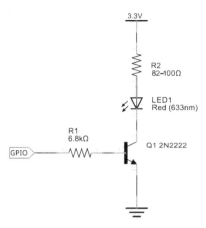

Assuming that you have this circuit constructed, or have some similar way of driving an LED, then a simple PWM program to modify its brightness from low to high and back to low in a loop is:

```
from gpiozero import PWMOutputDevice
from time import sleep

pwm=PWMOutputDevice(4)
pwm.frequency=1000
steps=8
delay=0.01
while True:
        for d in range(steps):
                pwm.value=d/steps
                sleep(delay)

        for d in range(steps):
                pwm.value=(steps-d)/steps
                sleep(delay)
```

The basic idea is to set up a pulse train with a period of 1ms. Next, in the for loop, the duty cycle is set to go from 0% to 100% and then back down to 0%.

You can achieve the same result using:

```
from gpiozero import PWMOutputDevice
pwm=PWMOutputDevice(4)
pwm.frequency=1000
pwm.pulse(fade_in_time=1,fade_out_time=1,n=None,background=False)
```

You might be thinking that the next thing to do is to create a PWMLED custom class. The good news is you don't have to as PWMLED is a standard class within GPIO Zero and has an identical set of methods to PWMOutputDevice. You can create a flashing LED with almost no effort:

```
from gpiozero import PWMLED
pwmLED=PWMLED(4)
pwmLED.pulse(fade_in_time=1,fade_out_time=1,
                              n=None,background=False)
```

If you want a full on and full off period then try:

```
from gpiozero import PWMLED
pwmLED=PWMLED(4)
pwmLED.blink(fade_in_time=1,on_time=2,fade_out_time=1,off_time=2,
                              n=None,background=False)
```

RGBLED

A simple variation on the PCWLED is the RGBLED. RGB LEDs are four-pin devices in which a red, a green and a blue LED are packaged into a single case. You can switch the three LEDs on and off independently. You can see a typical device below complete with its connections:

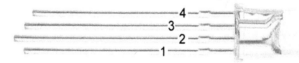

RGB LEDs come in two types, common anode (right) and common cathode (left), depending on which end of the LEDs makes the connection:

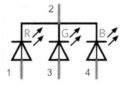 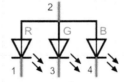

How to drive such an LED is just a repeat of driving a single LED. You need at the very least three current-limiting resistors:

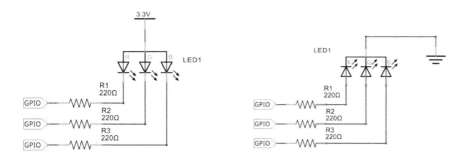

How you wire them up depends on whether the device is common cathode or common anode. The diagram on the left is for a common anode arrangement and in this case the LED lights up when the GPIO line is low. The diagram on the right is for common cathode and in this case the LED lights up when the GPIO line is high. If you want brighter LEDs then you will also need three transistors to drive them at a higher current. Also, in principle, each of the LEDs has a different forward voltage and so if you want them to be the same brightness you need to adjust the current-limiting resistors, but in practice this is rarely necessary.

Once you have the RGB LED wired up all you have to do is create an `RGBLED` object to control it. The simplest constructor call is just:

```
RGBLED(red,green,blue)
```

where red, green and blue are the GPIO lines controlling the color specified. Following on from this you can use the `color` method to specify which of the RGB LEDs is on. For example:

```
from gpiozero import RGBLED

led = RGBLED(2, 3, 4)
led.color = (1, 1, 0)
```

turns on the red and green LEDs, making yellow.

At this point you might be wondering where PWM comes into the picture. The answer is that the three LEDs in the `RGBLED` are `PWMLED` objects and this means that you can specify values between 0 and 1 in the `color` method. For example:

```
led.color = (0.5, 0.5, 0.5)
```

produces gray with each LED on 50% of the time.

If you use pwm=`False` in the constructor, three standard LEDs are used and you are restricted to `0` and `1` in the calls to the `color method`.

As long as you use pwm=`True`, the default, all of the `PWMLED` methods are available including `toggle`, `pulse` and `blink`. In each case the three LEDs are varied according to the color specified. For example:

```
pulse(fade_in_time=1, fade_out_time=1, on_color=(1, 1, 1),
                    off_color=(0, 0, 0), n=None, background=True)
```

will vary each LED from the specified off duty cycle to the specified on duty cycle in the specified `fade_in_time` and back to the off color in the `fade_out_time`.

It is worth knowing a little about how `RGBLED` works. It could make use of the `CompositeDevice` class, explained later, to create and manage three `PWMLED` devices or three ordinary LEDs, but instead it does the job directly and creates a tuple of the required LED objects. That is, assuming pwm=`True`, it creates a tuple equivalent to:

```
self._leds=tuple(PWMLED(red), PWMLED(green), PWMLED(blue))
```

The modified methods then work with this tuple of LED devices.

Tonal Buzzer

What if you want to produce not exactly music, but a tone at least. We have already looked at `Buzzer` back in Chapter 5. It is a simple on/off device – it either buzzes or it doesn't – and you can't modify the frequency. While in most cases it is the duty cycle that is important in the use of PWM, you can make use of it here to create a variable frequency output. In this case to hear the sound you need either a passive buzzer or a small loudspeaker. In either case, you will need a transistor driver, or even a full amplifier, to get a reasonable volume.

A passive buzzer is difficult to buy because they look the same as active buzzers and even buzzers that claim to be "passive" are in fact active. The difference between them is that when you connect an active buzzer to a power source it starts to buzz, usually very loudly, whereas a passive buzzer doesn't have any sound-generating electronics and needs a varying signal to make any sound. Most passive buzzers are piezoelectric and while these draw little current, they are not safe to simply connect to a GPIO line. There are also electromagnetic buzzers available in the same packaging and these have a very low resistance which would effectively short out a GPIO line connected directly, so proceed with caution. A small electromagnetic loudspeaker also has low resistance and needs to be driven by a transistor.

As far as the GPIO line is concerned, a passive piezoelectric buzzer looks like a capacitor and has to be driven in a way that allows it to charge and discharge. You can get away with connecting a piezoelectric buzzer directly, but you risk damaging the Pi in the long run and it won't be very loud.

The correct way to do the job is:

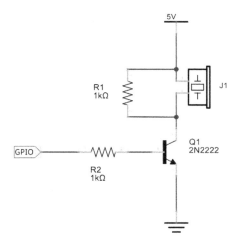

It is also worth knowing that piezoelectric buzzers make more noise at high frequency and usually have a high resonant frequency.

If you want to use a small loudspeaker then you need to know that even the smallest will draw more current than a GPIO line can safely supply. You can drive a speaker with a single transistor, but a push-pull arrangement is better, even if it does use two transistors:

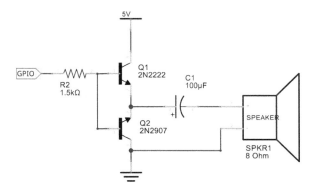

Alternatively you can use any audio amplifier you can find – there are many low-cost modules available.

Now we have the buzzer or speaker connected, the software is relatively easy. The `TonalBuzzer` class plus the `Tone` class gives you multiple ways to specify a note. You can construct a `Tone` object to specify the frequencies you want in a number of ways:

◆ `from_frequency(440)` or `Tone(frequency=440)`
  Specifies a frequency in Hz
◆ `from_note('A4')` or `Tone(note='A4')`
  Specifies a musical note giving the note name and octave
◆ `from_midi(69)` or `Tone(midi=69)`
  Produces the specified tone

If you simply use the constructor without saying what the specification method is then it does its best to work it out. So `Tone(440)` gives you a note with its frequency set to 440Hz, as does `Tone('A4')` and `Tone(69)`.

There are also some useful methods for working with notes:

◆ `down(n=m)`   Lowers note by m semitones
◆ `up(n=m)`   Raises note by m semitones
◆ `frequency()`   Returns current frequency
◆ `note()`   Returns the nearest note to the current frequency
◆ `midi()`   Return nearest midi note to the current frequency

Using them and `TonalBuzzer` we can easily write a program to produce a concert A, i.e. the note used to tune orchestras:

```
from gpiozero import TonalBuzzer
from signal import pause
tonal=TonalBuzzer(4)
tonal.play("A4")
pause()
```

If you try this out you will find that you do indeed get a noise that is about 440Hz. How pleasant you find the noise depends on the buzzer or speaker you are using and it isn't always the case that better equipment produces better sound. If you check on the frequency you will find the usual discrepancy between the specified and actual frequency. For example, a Pi Zero using `rpigpio` produces a note of 402Hz for A4 which is off by 38Hz, i.e. an error of just less than 9%.

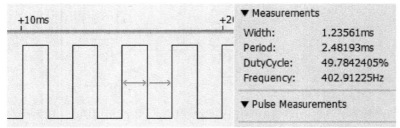

A Pi 5 using `lgpio` is much more accurate at about 439.9Hz.

144

Uses of PWM – D to A

So far we have looked at PWM driving devices that were happy being switched on and off and hence varying their output. Of course, an LED doesn't dim to 50%, it is simply off for half of the time and our eyes don't see the flashing as long as it is fast enough. It is possible to arrange for a PWM signal to generate a voltage proportional to its duty cycle and remove all the switching on and off. If you add a low-pass filter to the output of a PWM signal then what you get is the average of the voltage, i.e. a voltage that is proportional to the duty cycle.

This can be looked at in many different ways, but again it is the result of the amount of power delivered by a PWM signal. You can also think of it as using the filter to remove the high frequency components of the signal, leaving only the slower components, due to the modulation of the duty cycle.

The PWM output in this configuration mimics the workings of a digital to analog converter. You set the duty cycle d to a value between 0 to 1 and you get a voltage output that is 3.3 times dV. The frequency of the PWM signal governs how fast you can change the voltage. The usual rule of thumb is that you need 10 pulses to occur per conversion, i.e. the maximum frequency you can produce is pulse frequency/10. This means that the fastest signal you can create using the GPIO pin factory is around 1kHz, which isn't fast enough for a great many applications and you can't use it for sound synthesis, in particular.

To demonstrate the sort of approach that you can take to D to A conversion, the following program creates a triangle waveform:

```
from gpiozero import PWMOutputDevice
from time import sleep

pwm=PWMOutputDevice(4)
pwm.frequency=1000
steps=8
delay=0.001
while True:
    for d in range(steps):
        pwm.value=d/steps
        sleep(delay)

    for d in range(steps):
        pwm.value=(steps-d)/steps
        sleep(delay)
```

This first generates an increasing duty cycle and then a decreasing duty cycle with about 8 pulses needed to go from 0 to 1 and then back to 1.

To see the analog waveform, we need to put the digital output into a low-pass filter. A simple resistor and capacitor work reasonably well:

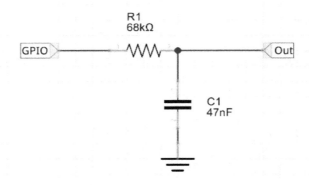

The filter's cutoff is 50Hz and might be a little on the high side for a frequency output this low.

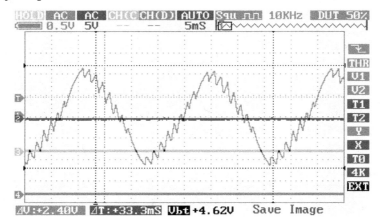

You can see that the frequency is around 43Hz and there are still lots of "jaggies" which could be further reduced by using a larger capacitor in the filter. There is a particularly big step at the start and end of each cycle, due to the jump to a duty cycle of 0 and 1. Nothing can be done about this.

You can create a sine wave, or any other waveform you need, using the same techniques, but 200Hz is a practical upper limit on what can be managed.

If you already know that the PWM outputs are used to create audio on the Pi, you might be wondering how this is possible? The answer is that it uses hardware-generated PWM and can reach much higher frequencies.

What Else Can You Use PWM For?

PWM lines are incredibly versatile and it is always worth asking the question "could I use PWM?" when you are considering almost any problem. The LED example shows how you can use PWM as a power controller. You can extend this idea to a computer-controlled switch mode power supply. All you need is a capacitor to smooth out the voltage and perhaps a transformer to change the voltage.

You can also use PWM to control the speed of a DC motor, the subject of the next chapter, and if you add a simple bridge circuit you can control its direction and speed.

Finally, you can use a PWM signal as a modulated carrier for data communications. For example, most infrared controllers make use of a 38kHz carrier, which is roughly a $26\mu s$ pulse. This is switched on and off for 1ms and this is well within the range that the PWM can manage. So all you have to do is replace the red LED in the previous circuit with an infrared LED and you have the start of a remote control, or data transmission, link.

Summary

- PWM, Pulse Width Modulation, has a fixed repetition rate, but a variable duty cycle, i.e. the amount of time the signal is high or low changes.

- PWM can be generated by software simply by changing the state of a GPIO line correctly, but it can also be generated in hardware, so relieving the processor of some work.

- As well as being a way of signaling, PWM can also be used to vary the amount of power or voltage transferred. The higher the duty cycle, the more power/voltage.

- The Pi has two hardware PWM lines and these are capable of a range of operational modes, but GPIO Zero only supports software-generated PWM at the moment.

- The fundamental PWM class is `PWMOutputDevice` and, although it seems not to be intended for regular use, it is very easy to use it for raw PWM.

- By varying the duty cycle, you can dim an LED using `PWMOutputDevice` but it isn't very accurate on frequency or duty cycle.

- There is also a `PWMLED` which can vary the brightness of an LED.

- The `RGBLED` class uses three `PWMLED` to create any color.

- `TonalBuzzer` uses PWM to vary the frequency.

- PWM can be used to implement a D to A converter simply by varying the duty cycle and by varying the output of the D to A you can create music.

Chapter 11

Controlling Motors And Servos

Motors form an important class of output devices and they are fairly easy to use, but it is important to understand the different types of motor that you can use.

The simplest division among types of motor are AC and DC. AC motors are generally large and powerful and run from mains voltage. As they are more difficult to work with, and they work at mains voltages, these aren't used much in IoT applications. DC motors generally work on lower voltage and are much more suitable for the IoT. In this chapter we will only look at DC motors and how they work thanks to pulse width modulation.

DC Motor

There are two big classes of DC motors – brushed and brushless. All motors work by using a set of fixed magnets, the stator, and a set of rotating magnets, the rotor. The important idea is that a motor generates a "push" that rotates the shaft by the forces between the magnet that makes up the stator and the magnet that makes up the rotor. The stronger these magnets are, the stronger the push and the more torque (turning force) the motor can produce. To keep the motor turning, one of the two magnetic fields has to change to keep the rotor being attracted to a new position.

DC motors differ in how they create the magnetism in each component, either using a permanent magnet or an electromagnet. This means there are four possible arrangements:

	1	2	3	4
Stator	Permanent	Permanent	Electromagnet	Electromagnet
Rotor	Permanent	Electromagnet	Permanent	Electromagnet
Type	Can't work	Brushed DC	Brushless DC	Series or shunt

Arrangement 1 can't produce a motor because there is no easy way of changing the magnetic field. Arrangement 4 produces the biggest and most powerful DC motors as used in trains, cars and so on. Arrangement 2, Brushed DC, is the most commonly encountered form of "small" DC motor. However, arrangement 3, brushless DC, is becoming increasingly popular.

Different arrangements produce motors which have different torque characteristics – i.e. how hard they are to stop at any given speed. Some types of motor are typically low torque at any speed, i.e. they spin fast but are easy to stop.

Low torque motors are often used with gearboxes which reduce the speed and increase the torque. The big problem with gearboxes, apart from extra cost, is backlash. The gears don't mesh perfectly and this looseness means that you can turn the input shaft and at first the output shaft won't move. Only when the slack in the gears has been taken up will the output shaft move. This makes a geared motor less useful for precise positioning, although there are ways to improve on this using feedback and clever programming.

Brushed Motors

To energize the electromagnets, a brushed motor supplies current to the armature via a split ring or commutator and brushes. As the rotor rotates, the current in the coil is reversed and it is always attracted to the other pole of the magnet.

The only problem with this arrangement is that, as the brushes rub on the slip ring as the armature rotates, they wear out and cause sparks and hence RF interference. The quality of a brushed motor depends very much on the design of the brushes and the commutator.

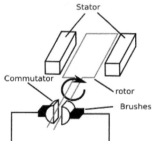

Very small, cheap, brushed DC motors, of the sort in the picture below, tend to not have brushes that can be changed and when they wear out the motor has to be replaced. They also tend to have very low torque and high speed. This usually means that they have to be used with a gearbox. If you overload a brushed motor then the tendency is to demagnetize the stator magnets. The cheapest devices are basically toys.

150

Higher quality brushed motors are available and they also come in a variety of form factors. For example, the 775 motor measures 66.7mm by 42mm overall with a 5mm shaft:

Even these motors tend not to have user serviceable brushes, but they generally last a long time due to better construction.

Unidirectional Brushed Motor

A brushed motor can be powered by simply connecting it to a DC supply. Reversing the DC supply reverses the direction of the motor. The speed is simply proportional to the applied voltage. If all you want is a unidirectional control then all you need is a PWM driver that can supply the necessary current and voltage.

A single transistor solution is workable as long as you include a diode to allow the energy stored in the windings to discharge when the motor is rotating, but not under power:

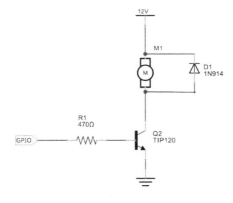

This circuit is simple and will work with motor voltages up to 40V and motor currents up to 5A continuous, 8A peak. The only small point to note is that the TIP120 is a Darlington pair, i.e. it is two transistors in the same case, and as such the base voltage drop is twice the usual 0.6V, i.e. 1.2V, and this has to be taken into account when calculating the current-limiting resistor.

It is sometimes said that the TIP120 and similar are inefficient power controllers because, comprising two transistors, they have twice the emitter collector voltage you would expect, which means they dissipate more power than necessary. If you are running a motor from a battery you might want to use a MOSFET, but as described earlier 3.3V is low to switch a MOSFET on and off. One solution is to use a BJT to increase the voltage applied to the gate:

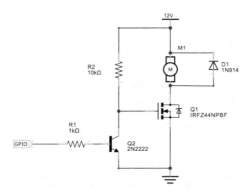

The BJT connects the gate to 12V. As the IRFZ44NPBF has a threshold voltage between 2V and 4V devices should work at 5V and sometimes at 3.3V without the help of the BJT, but providing 12V ensures that the MOSFET is fully on. One problem with the circuit is that the use of the BJT inverts the signal. When the GPIO line is high the BJT is on and the MOSFET is off and vice versa. In other words, GPIO line high switches the motor off and low switches it on. This MOSFET can work with voltages up to 50V and currents of 40A. The 2N2222 can only work at 30V, or 40V in the case of the 2N2222A.

A third approach to controlling a unidirectional motor is to use half an H-bridge. Why this is so-called, and why you might want to do it, will become apparent in the next section on bidirectional motors. Half an H-bridge makes use of two complementary devices, either an NPN and a PNP BJT or an N- and P-type MOSFET. For example:

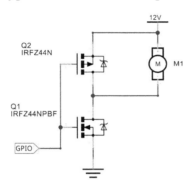

If the GPIO line is high then Q1 is on and Q2 off and the motor runs. If the GPIO line is low then Q1 is off and Q2 is on and the motor is braked – it has a resistance to rotating because of the back EMF generated when the rotor turns. You probably need a BJT to feed the MOSFETs as selected.

There is no GPIO Zero class to control a unidirectional motor, but it is easy to create one from PWMOutputDevice:

```
class uniMotor(PWMOutputDevice):
    def __init__(self, pin=None, active_high=True,
                        initial_value=0,pin_factory=None):
        super(uniMotor, self).__init__(
            pin, active_high, initial_value,
pin_factory=pin_factory
            )
    def speed(self,value):
        self._write(value)

motor=uniMotor(4)
motor.speed(0.5)
sleep(10)
```

We have simply added a speed method. The inherited methods on and off are still useful, but it might be better to block access to pulse and blink. Also notice that if you are using the transistor/MOSFET driver, then setting active_high=False solves the need to provide an inverted pulse.

Bidirectional Brushed Motor

If you want bidirectional control then you need to use an H-bridge:

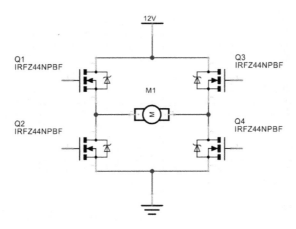

It is easy to see how this works. If Q1 and Q4 are the only MOSFETs on the motor, + is connected to 12V and – to ground. The motor runs in the forward direction. If Q2 and Q3 are the only MOSFETs on the motor, + is connected to ground and – is connected to 12V. The motor runs in the reverse direction. Of course, if none or any one is on the motor is off. If Q1 and Q3, or Q2 and Q4, are on then the motor is braked as its windings are shorted out and the back EMF acts as a brake.

You can arrange to drive the four MOSFETs using four GPIO lines - just make sure that they switch on and off in the correct order. Alternatively, you can add a NOT gate to each pair so that you switch Q1/Q2 and Q3/ Q4 to opposite states.

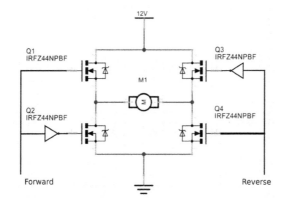

An alternative design is to use complementary MOSFETs:

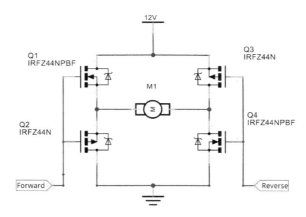

In this configuration, the first GPIO line drives the motor forward and the second drives it in reverse. The effect of setting the two lines is:

Forward	Reverse	Motor
Low	Low	Off
Low	High	Reverse
High	Low	Forward
High	High	Braked

You can also drive the GPIO lines for Forward/Reverse with a PWM signal and control the motor's speed as well as direction. If you use the MOSFETs shown in the diagram then you would also need a BJT to increase the drive voltage to each MOSFET, as in the unidirectional case. You also need to include diodes to deal with potential reverse voltage on each of the MOSFETs. The most important thing about an H-bridge is that Q1/Q2 and Q3/Q4 should never be on together – this would short circuit the power supply.

If working with four BJTs or MOSFETs is more than you want to tackle, the good news is that there are chips that implement two H-bridges per device. You can also buy low-cost, ready-made, modules with one or more H-bridges.

One of the most used devices is the L298 Dual H-bridge which works up to 46V and total DC current of 4A.

The block diagram of one of the two H-bridges shows exactly how it works.

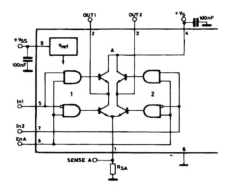

You can see that the bridge is made up of four BJTs and there are logic gates to allow In1 and In2 to select the appropriate pairs of devices. The only extras are AND gates and that the EnA line is used to switch all of the transistors off. The line shown as Sense A can be used to detect the speed or load of the motor, but is rarely used.

A typical module based on the L298 can be seen below.

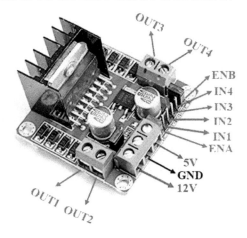

It is easier to describe how to use this sort of module with a single motor. The motor is connected to OUT1 and OUT2. Three GPIO lines are connected to ENA, IN1 and IN2. ENA is an enable line, which has to be high for the motor to run at all. IN1 and IN2 play the role of direction control lines – which one is forward and which is reverse depends on which way round you connect the motor. Putting a PWM signal on to ENA controls the speed of the motor and this allows IN1 and IN2 to be simple digital outputs.

Notice that the power connector shows 5V and 12V supplies, but most of these modules have a voltage regulator which will reduce the 12V to 5V. In this case you don't have to supply a 5V connection. If you want to use more than 12V then the regulator has to be disconnected and you need to arrange for a separate 5V supply – check with the module's documentation. Notice that the transistors in the bridge have around a 2V drop, so using 12V results in just 10V being applied to the motor.

Another very popular H-bridge device is the SN754410 driver. This is suitable for smaller, lower powered, motors and it has two complete H-bridges. It can supply up to 1A per driver and work from 4.5 to 36V. It has the same set of control lines as the L298, i.e. each motor has a Forward/Reverse control line and an Enable. You don't have to use the Enable line; it can be connected to +5V to allow PWM to be applied on the Forward/Reverse lines.

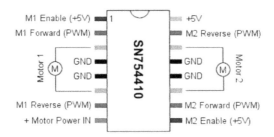

Motor Software

There is a specific GPIO Zero class, `Motor`, to control a motor using an H-bridge module of this sort. It seems to have been written with the idea that an H-bridge would only support the Forward and Reverse control lines and not the Enable. The basic constructor is:

```
Motor(forward, backward, pwm=True)
```

The GPIO lines Forward and Reverse have to be connected to the IN1/IN2 or IN3/IN4. You also need to connect ENA or ENB to +5V to enable the motor. If you use the default `pwm=True` then the GPIO lines supply a PWM signal with a duty cycle set by you to control the motor's speed. If you don't use

PWM then you can simply turn the motor on and off in the direction you want. If you want to use the Enable connection then you have to use:

```
Motor(forward, backward,enable=pinnum, pwm=True)
```

In this case you have to connect the GPIO line specified by `enable` to the ENA or the ENB line. The `Motor` class doesn't use the enable line for a PWM signal, it simply sets it high or low. The disadvantage of this arrangement is that three GPIO lines are used. The advantage is that you don't have to arrange for the ENA and/or ENB lines to be physically set high.

Once you have a `Motor` object:

```
motor=Motor(4,14)
```

which assumes that you are using GPIO4 and GPIO14 for IN1 and IN2 and have connected ENA to 5V, you can use:

```
motor.backward(duty)
motor.forward(duty)
```

to set the motor moving in the given direction and a speed specified by the duty cycle. You can also use:

```
motor.reverse()
```

to reverse the direction without changing the speed and:

```
motor.stop()
```

to stop the motor.

You can also set the motor's direction and speed using its `value` property. This can be set to a value in the range `-1` to `1` for full reverse to full forward.

There are H-bridges that use two lines to control Phase and Enable. These map to the usual Forward, Reverse and Enable as shown below:

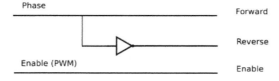

The disadvantage of this arrangement is that you cannot set Forward and Reverse to one to put the motor into brake mode. If you do have this sort of controller, anything based on the MAX14870/2 for example, then you can use the `PhaseEnabledMotor` class:

```
PhaseEnableMotor(phase,enable)
```

where `phase` is the GPIO line use to control direction and `enable` is the GPIO line that generates the PWM signal. This has the same methods as the `Motor` class and is used in the same way. By default it uses PWM for the Enable line unless you set `pwm=False` in the constructor.

Using Full H-Bridge As Two Half H-Bridges

It is easy to think of an H-bridge as being only for bidirectional control, but each full bridge is composed of two half bridges and this means a typical dual full H-bridge can control four unidirectional motors:

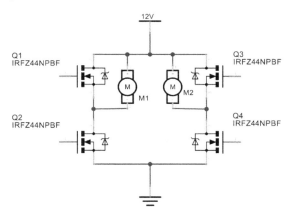

In this case Forward is now MotorM1 speed control and Reverse is now MotorM2 speed control. Any enable line has to be set high to allow the two motors to be controlled. You can make use of this arrangement in software simply by instantiating two uniMotor objects – one on the forward line and one on the reverse:

```
motorA=uniMotor(4)
motorB=uniMotor(14)
motorA.speed(0.5)
motorB.speed(0.3)
sleep(10)
```

Here motorA is connected to GPIO4, which is in turn connected to Forward and motorB is connected to GPIO14, which is in turn connected to Reverse.

Controlling a Servo

Hobby servos, of the sort used in radio control models, are very cheap and easy to use and they connect via a standard PWM protocol. Servos are not drive motors, but positioning motors. That is, they don't rotate at a set speed, they move to a specified angle or position.

A servo is a motor, usually a brushed DC motor, with a feedback sensor for position, usually a simple variable resistor (potentiometer) connected to the shaft. The output is usually via a set of gears which reduces the rotation rate and increases the torque. The motor turns the gears, and hence the shaft, until the potentiometer reaches the desired setting and hence the shaft has the required angle/position.

A basic servo has just three connections, ground, a power line and a signal line. The colors used vary, but the power line is usually red, ground is usually black or brown and the signal line is white, yellow or orange. If a standard J connector is fitted then the wire nearest the notch, pin 3, is Signal, that in the middle, pin 2, is 5V and outer, pin 1, is Ground.

The power wire has to be connected to a 5V supply capable of providing enough current to run the motor - anything up to 500mA or more depending on the servo. In general, you cannot power a full-size servo from the Pi's 5V pin, you need a separate power supply. You can power some micro servos directly from the Pi's 5V line, but you need to check the specifications. The good news is that the servo's signal line generally needs very little current, although it does need to be switched between 0 and 5V using a PWM signal.

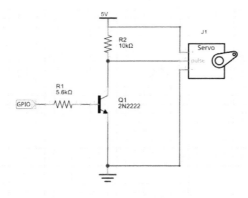

We can assume that the signal line needs to be driven as a voltage load and so the appropriate way to drive the servo is:

- ◆ The servo's + line needs to be connected to an external 5V power supply, unless it is a micro servo when it might be possible to power it from the Pi's 5V line.

- ◆ The 10K resistor R1 can be a lot larger for most servos - 47K often works. The 5.6K resistor limits the base current to slightly less than 0.5mA.

Notice, however, that if you are using a single BJT driver, like the one shown above, the input is inverted.

This is the correct way to drive a servo, but in nearly all cases you can drive the servo signal line directly from the 3.3V GPIO line with a 1K resistor to limit the current if anything goes wrong with the servo. Some servos will even work with their motor connected to 3.3V, but at much reduced torque. The Pi cannot supply enough current in this configuration, so use a 5V supply for the motor.

Now all we have to do is set the PWM line to produce 20ms pulses with pulse widths ranging from 0.5ms to 2.5ms.

The GPIO Zero `Servo` class makes it easy to work with almost any servo on any GPIO line that the pin factory supports:

```
Servo(pin,initial_value=0, min_pulse_width=1/1000,
                max_pulse_width=2/1000, frame_width=20/1000)
```

The `min_pulse_width` and `max_pulse_width` can be used to limit the movement of the servo and `frame_width` gives that repeat rate for the signal, which in most cases is 20ms or 50Hz.

The simplest servo program you can write is something like:

```
from gpiozero import Servo
from time import sleep

servo = Servo(4)

while True:
    servo.min()
    sleep(0.5)
    servo.mid()
    sleep(0.5)
    servo.max()
    sleep(0.5)
```

This moves the servo to three positions, `min`, `mid` and `max`, pausing between each. If you want to move the servo to an intermediate position, simply set its value property to something in the range -1 to 1 corresponding to min to max positions.

If you run the program using the circuit given earlier, you will discover that the servo does nothing at all, apart perhaps from vibrating. The reason is that the transistor voltage driver is an inverter. When the PWM line is high the transistor is fully on and the servo's pulse line is effectively grounded. When the PWM line is low the transistor is fully off and the servo's pulse line is pulled high by the resistor.

The obvious solution to this problem is to set `active_high` to `False` to invert the working of the GPIO line, but `Servo` doesn't support `active_high` in its constructor. In principle, you can set:

```
servo.pwm_device.active_high=False
```

after the constructor, but this doesn't work as `Servo` works directly with the pin rather than the `value` property of `PWMOutputDevice`, which bypasses `active_high`.

The simplest solution is to create a new class and override the value property setter:

```
from gpiozero import Servo

class ServoInvert(Servo):
@Servo.value.setter
  def value(self, value):
    if value is None:
     self.pwm_device.pin.frequency = None
    elif -1 <= value <= 1:
     self.pwm_device.pin.frequency = int(1 / self.frame_width)
     self.pwm_device.value = (self._min_dc + self._dc_range *
                   ((value - self._min_value) / self._value_range))
    else:
     raise OutputDeviceBadValue(
             "Servo value must be between -1 and 1, or None")
```

The only line changed from the original code is:

```
self.pwm_device.value = (self._min_dc + self._dc_range *
                  ((value - self._min_value) / self._value_range))
```

Now you can use `ServoInvert` with a one-transistor driver:

```
servo = ServoInvert(4)
servo.pwm_device.active_high=False
```

Notice that in either case if the servo doesn't move over its full range when you go from max to min you can adjust `min_pulse_width` and `max_pulse_width`. The values given are for a typical servo.

As well as the simple `Servo` class there is also the `AngularServo` class:

```
AngularServo(pin,initial_angle=0,min_angle=-90,max_angle=90,
           min_pulse_width=1/1000, max_pulse_width=2/1000,
           frame_width=20/1000)
```

This works in the same way as the `Servo` class, but you can calibrate the servo to work in terms of angles. Simply measure the angle from the mid position that you get for the `max` and `min` servo positions and specify them in `min_angle` and `max_angle`. For example, if you measure the max position as being 60 degrees from the mid position and the min position to be 75 degrees, you could create a calibrated `AngularServo` using:

```
servo = AngularServo(4, min_angle=-75, max_angle=60)
```

and after this you can use the `angle` method to move to a specified angle:

```
servo.angle(25)
```

which moves the servo 25 degrees towards the maximum position.

The task of calibrating a servo, determining what duty cycle is needed to make it move to each of its extreme positions, is something that you should always do.

It is worth mentioning that servos make good low-cost DC motors complete with gearboxes. All you have to do is open the servo, unsolder the motor from the control circuits and solder two wires to the motor. If you want to use the forward/reverse electronics you can remove the end stops on the gearbox, usually on the large gearwheel and replace the potentiometer with a pair of equal value resistors – 2.2kΩ, say.

Brushless DC Motors

Brushless DC motors are more expensive than brushed DC motors, but they are superior in many ways. They don't fail because of commutator or brush wear and need no maintenance. They provide maximum rotational torque at all points of the rotation and generally provide more power for the same size and weight. They can also be controlled more precisely. The only negative points are higher cost and slightly more complex operation. In practice, it is usually better to use a brushed DC motor unless you really need something extra.

A brushless DC motor is basically a brushed motor turned inside out – the stator is a set of electromagnets and the rotor is a set of permanent magnets. In some designs the permanent magnets are inside the stator in the manner of a brushed motor – an inrunner – and sometimes the magnets are outside of the stator – an outrunner.

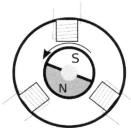

An inrunner – the permanent magnets form the rotor and the coils are switched to attract.

163

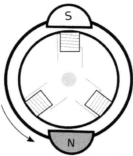

An outrunner – the permanent magnets are on the outside of the stator and the whole cover rotates.

A brushless motor works in exactly the same way as a brushed motor. As the coils are stationary there is no need for a mechanical commutator, but there is still need for commutation – the coils have to be switched on in sequence to create a rotating magnetic field which pulls the rotor around with it. This means that you have to implement an electronic commutator, which is another name for brushless DC motors.

An electronic commutator has to sense the position of the rotor and change the magnetic field generated by the stator to keep the rotor moving. Brushless motors differ in the number of magnets they have – the number of poles and the number of electromagnets – and the number of phases. The most common is a three-phase motor as these are used in radio control modeling. Essentially you need at least a driver for each of the phases and a GPIO line to generate the signal. In practice, you need two drivers for each phase and they have to be driven from a dual supply so that the magnetic field can be positive, zero or negative.

This would be possible to do with software, but it isn't easy and with the given that GPIO Zero is currently limited to software-generated PWM, this would be to slow and unreliable. A more reasonable alternative is to buy a ready-built controller. There are two types of brushless motor – with Hall sensors and without. The ones with sensors are more expensive, but easier to control because the electronics always knows where the rotor is and can apply the correct drive. The ones without sensors are controlled by measuring the back EMF from the motor and this is much harder. Most of the lower cost speed controllers need motors with Hall sensors.

The radio control community has taken to using three-phase brushless motors and this has resulted in a range of motors and controllers at reasonable prices. The problem is that they are intended as high-power, high-speed, unidirectional motors for use in quadcopters and model planes.

If you can live with their limitations they provide a good way to couple a Pi to a brushless motor. In this case all you need is a three-phase brushless motor of the sort used in RC modeling and an ESC (Electronic Speed Controller) of the sort shown below:

The three leads on the left go to the three phases of the motor and the red and black leads on the right go to a power supply – often a LiPo battery. The small three-wire connector in the middle is a standard servo connector and you can use it exactly as if the brushless motor was a servo, with a few exceptions. The first is that the middle pin 2 supplies 5V rather than accepts it. Don't connect this to anything unless you want a 5V supply. The second problem is that ESCs are intelligent. When you first apply power they beep and can be programmed into different modes by changing the PWM signal from max to min. Also, to use an ESC you have to arm it. This is to avoid radio control modelers from being injured by motors that start unexpectedly when the power is applied. The most common arming sequence is for the ESC to beep when power is applied. You then have to set the PWM to min, when the ESC will beep again. After a few moments you will have control of the motor.

The need for an arming procedure should alert you to the fact that these model motors are very powerful. Don't try working with one loose on the bench as it will move fast if switched on and at the very least make a twisted mess of your wires. Most importantly of all, don't run a motor with anything attached until you have everything under control.

Stepper Motors

There is one sort of brushless motor that is easy to use and low cost – the stepper motor. This differs from a standard brushless motor in that it isn't designed for continuous high-speed rotation. A stepper motor has an arrangement of magnets and coils such that powering some of the coils holds the rotor in a particular position. Changing which coils are activated makes the rotor turn until it is aligned with the coils and stops moving. Thus the stepper motor moves the rotor in discrete steps. This makes driving it much simpler.

Stepper motors have no brushes and so don't wear out as fast as brushed motors. They also have roughly the same torque at any speed and can be used at low speeds without a gearbox. They can remain in a fixed position for a long time without burning out, as DC motors would. Unlike a servo, however, if a stepper motor is mechanically forced to a new position, it will not return to its original position when released. The only disadvantage of a stepper motor is that the continuous rotation produced by repeated stepping can make the motor vibrate.

Stepper motors vary in the size of a step they use – typically 1.8 degrees giving 200 steps per rotation, although gearing can be used to reduce the step size. Another big difference is what the rotor is made up of – permanent magnets or soft iron. The first type is called a PM stepper and the second, or VR stepper, standing for Variable Reluctance, and they differ in how you drive them. PM steppers are easier to understand. There are also hybrid steppers which share the good characteristics of both PM and VR stepper motors. These are more expensive and generally only used where accuracy of positioning is important.

They also differ in the number of phases i.e. independent banks of coils they have. The diagram below shows a two-phase PM stepper motor with Phase 1 activated:

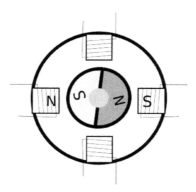

If Phase two is activated, the rotor turns through 90 degrees:

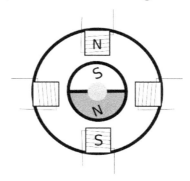

This is the simplest stepper motor you can make. A typical stepper motor will have many more coils than four, but they are usually connected into two or three phases.

Another big difference is bipolar versus unipolar. A bipolar motor is like the one shown in the diagram. To generate a north pole the current has to flow in the opposite direction to when you want to create a south pole. This means you have to drive each bank of coils with a bidirectional driver, e.g. an H-bridge. A unipolar motor has two windings, one in each direction, and both windings can be driven by a unidirectional driver – one giving a north pole and the other a south pole. Notice that a unipolar motor has twice the number of coils to drive and the switching sequence is slightly different.

A two-phase bipolar motor with Phases A and B would switch on in the sequence:

A → B → A- → B- → A etc

where the minus sign means the current flows the other way.

A two-phase unipolar motor has two coils per phase, A1, A2 and B1, B2

with the 1 and 2 windings creating opposite magnetic fields for the same current flow. Now the sequence is:

A1 → B1 → A2 → B2 → A1 etc

and all driven in the same direction.

Switching single phases fully on and off in sequence makes the motor make repeated steps. You can also switch on more than one phase at a time to generate micro-steps. For example, in our two-phase example, switching on two phases makes the rotor settle between the two, so producing a half micro-step:

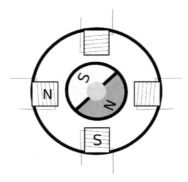

The driving sequence for a two-phase bipolar motor is:

A → AB →B → BA- → A- → A- B- → B- → AB- → A

with minus indicating that the coil is energized in the opposite direction, giving a total of eight, rather than four, steps.

You can even vary the current through the coils and move the rotor to intermediate positions. At the extreme limit you can vary the current sinusoidally and produce a smooth rotation. Micro-stepping is smoother and can eliminate buzzing. For high accuracy positioning, micro-stepping is a poor performer under load.

Stepper Motor Driver

How best to drive a stepper motor using a Pi?

There are stepper motor controllers, including HATs, that you can buy and these come with software that allows you to control the stepper. There are also some chips that work with unipolar and bipolar stepper motors. However, you can easily control a bipolar stepper motor using one of the H-bridges described in the section on directional motor control.

For example, using complementary MOSFETS:

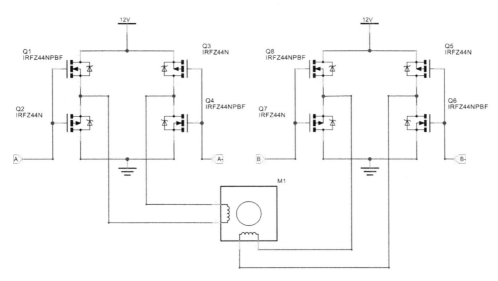

You can use a dual H-bridge module in the same way if you don't want to build it from scratch. The motor has to be a bipolar two-phase motor, often called a four-wire stepper motor. You can see that for this arrangement you need four GPIO lines, A, A-, B and B-.

What about driving the dual H-bridge using software? There is no Stepper motor class in GPIO Zero, but it is easy to create one. For this example the class we create doesn't integrate with GPIO Zero very well, but it works. In the next chapter we will discover how to do the job a little better.

Our new class is called StepperBi4 to indicate that it is a 4-wire bipolar stepper. You can make similar classes for unipolar steppers and for more phases:

```
class StepperBi4():
  def __init__(self, A=None,Am=None,B=None,Bm=None):
    self.phase=0
    self.gpios=tuple(DigitalOutputDevice(pin) for pin
                                   in (A,B,Am,Bm))
    self.halfstepSeq = [
                        [1,0,0,0],
                        [1,1,0,0],
                        [0,1,0,0],
                        [0,1,1,0],
                        [0,0,1,0],
                        [0,0,1,1],
                        [0,0,0,1],
                        [1,0,0,1]
                       ]
```

You can see that the constructor lets you specify the four GPIO lines driving the H-bridges – A positive and minus and B positive and minus. It keeps track of the current phase and sets up four `DigitalOutputDevice` instances, one for each GPIO line as a tuple. Notice that the order of the GPIO lines in the tuple is A,B,Am,Bm as this makes the phase table easier. The table gives the state of each GPIO line for each phase state. You can compare this to the sequence given earlier:

A → AB → B → BA- → A- → A-B- → B- → AB- → A

Now all we need are some methods to set and work with the phase:

```
def setPhase(self,phase):
    self.phase=phase
    for gpio,state in zip(self.gpios, self.halfstepSeq[phase]):
        gpio.value=state

def stepForward(self):
    self.phase=(self.phase+1) % 8
    self.setPhase(self.phase)

def stepReverse(self):
    self.phase=(self.phase-1) % 8
    self.setPhase(self.phase)
```

The only complicated part of this code is the use of `zip` to put together the gpio tuple and the appropriate line from the phase table. The result allows us to step through getting each `gpio` object and its new state in turn. The `stepForward` and `stepReverse` simply move down or up in the phase table, making sure to go back to the start when the end is reached. This is what the modulus operator, %, does for us and `phase` follows the sequence 0,1,2,3,4,5,6,7,0,1 and so on.

You can use a full step table if you want to as long as you remember to work in mod 4 rather than 8:

```
    self.fullstepSeq = [
            [1, 0, 0, 0],
            [0, 1, 0, 0],
            [0, 0, 1, 0],
            [0, 0, 0, 1],
        ]
```

```
    def setPhase(self, phase):
        self.phase = phase
        for gpio, state in zip(self.gpios,
                        self.fullstepSeq[phase]):
            gpio.pin._set_state(state)

    def stepForward(self):
        self.phase = (self.phase+1) % 4
        self.setPhase(self.phase)

    def stepReverse(self):
        self.phase = (self.phase-1) % 4
        self.setPhase(self.phase)
```

Putting all this together, we can write a program that rotates the stepper at a constant speed:

```
from gpiozero import DigitalOutputDevice
from time import sleep

class StepperBi4():
    def __init__(self, A=None,Am=None,B=None,Bm=None):
        self.phase=0
        self.gpios=
            tuple(DigitalOutputDevice(pin) for pin in (A,B,Am,Bm))
        self.halfstepSeq = [
                            [1,0,0,0],
                            [1,1,0,0],
                            [0,1,0,0],
                            [0,1,1,0],
                            [0,0,1,0],
                            [0,0,1,1],
                            [0,0,0,1],
                            [1,0,0,1]
                            ]
    def setPhase(self,phase):
        self.phase=phase
        for gpio,state in zip(self.gpios, self.halfstepSeq[phase]):
            gpio.value=state

    def stepForward(self):
        self.phase=(self.phase+1) % 8
        self.setPhase(self.phase)

    def stepReverse(self):
        self.phase=(self.phase-1) % 8
        self.setPhase(self.phase)
step=StepperBi4(4,17,27,22)
step.setPhase(0)
while True:
    sleep(0.001)
    step.stepForward()
```

In this case, H-bridge A is connected to GPIO4 and GPIO17 and B is connected to GPIO27 and GPIO22. The stepping speed is such that a 200-step motor will rotate at 2.5rpm which is a good starting point. Decrease the sleep time for a higher speed.

If you are using one of the many dual H-bridge modules then the wiring is as shown below:

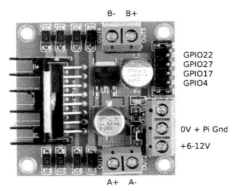

Notice that you have to connect the ground of the power supply and the Pi's ground together. It is also a good idea to use a power supply with a current trip when first trying things out.

You might think that the problem is that you cannot generate pulses fast enough, but the real problem is the variation in the time taken for a step. For example, rotating at 25rpm, still quite slow, we have a set of waveforms that look like:

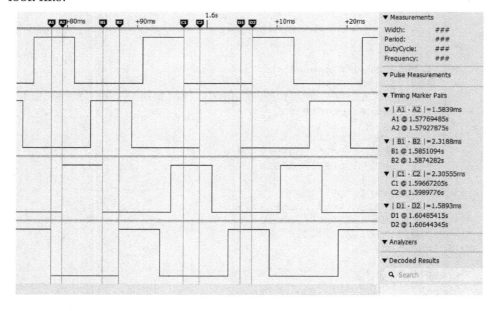

Marked on the logic analyzer trace are the times for a single line to be high, i.e. all the even states. The times for each are shown on the right and you can see the time for a half step varies between 1.6 to 2.3ms. This will cause the motor to vibrate as the speed increases.

In Chapter 6 we discovered that writing direct to a pin was ten times faster. If you change the `setPhase` method to:

```
def setPhase(self,phase):
    self.phase=phase
    for gpio,state in zip(self.gpios, self.halfstepSeq[phase]):
        gpio.pin._set_state(state)
```

the stability of the half step time improves:

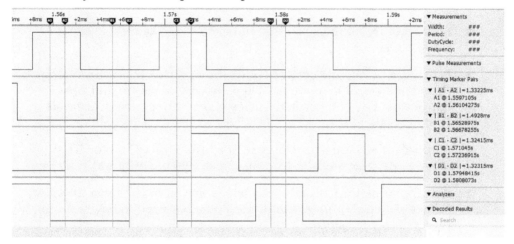

You can see now that, at the same frequency, the half step time varies from 1.32 to 1.49 ms, which produces a smoother rotation.

There are many other improvements that can be made to `StepperBi4` – additional methods for continuous rotation, a reverse method and so on, but this is all you need to use a stepper motor. You can also produce custom classes for other types of motor. All you need is the set of GPIO lines and the switching sequence.

If you need a stepper motor to turn at a given speed then this implementation isn't so good. The reason is simply that when the operating system interrupts the program there will be an irregularity in the pulse stream. If you run the motor at a steady step rate, you will notice the occasional change in speed of rotation. However, the system works well when it is only the number of steps that is at issue, as no steps are lost due to interruption. This makes it possible to use GPIO Zero to position something with a stepper motor, which is what they are mostly used for.

Summary

- There are a number of different types of electric motor, but DC brushed or brushless motors are the most used in the IoT.

- Brushed motors can be speed controlled using a single transistor driver and a PWM signal. There is no unidirectional motor class in GPIO Zero, but it is easy to create one.

- For bidirectional control you need an H-bridge. The Motor class can be used to control the direction and speed of a motor with the help of an H-bridge.

- Servo motors set their position in response to the duty cycle of a PWM signal.

- Brushless DC motors are very powerful and best controlled using off-the-shelf electronic modules. They are very powerful and thus dangerous if used incorrectly. They can be driven using a simple PWM signal.

- Stepper motors are a special case of a brushless DC motor. They move in discrete steps in response to energizing different coils.

- A unipolar motor has coils that can be driven in the same direction for every step. A bipolar motor has coils that need to be driven in reverse for some steps.

- Bipolar motors need two H-bridges to operate and four GPIO lines.

- There is no stepper motor class in GPIO Zero, but it is possible to create one.

Chapter 12

Working With Compound Devices

You might well start off with a single GPIO line flashing an LED, but slowly and surely you will graduate to more elaborate devices such as a robot that consists of a number of flashing LEDs, motors and so on. If what you have created is a development on an existing device then you might create a new custom class using inheritance and we have seen examples of this in earlier chapters. For example, when we wanted to implement a door lock class, the obvious way was to create a new class that inherited from the existing LED class. The reason is that both the LED and lock share a basic on/off behavior, but in the case of the lock it is better called "lock/unlock".

Compare this to the problem of building a custom class to control three or more separate LEDs. In this case you don't need to inherit the behavior of a single LED, you need multiple instances of the LED class. In this case what you need is composition, i.e. combining classes, rather than inheritance. GPIO Zero has a class that you can use to create composite devices and this chapter looks at how this works in enough detail for you to create your own.

Devices That Contain Devices

The CompositeDevice class is intended to be inherited by your custom classes to make it easy to include instances of other classes, but first it makes sense to see how to do the job without help.

If you were implementing a composite device from scratch then the logical thing to do is to create a tuple, list or dictionary of the instances you need. For example, if you wanted to create a custom TriLED class, you might write in the constructor a tuple like:

```
self.LEDs=(LED(pin1),LED(pin2),LED(pin3))
```

After this you would write the methods that are required using the tuple to access the LEDs.

For example, you might want an AllOn and AllOff method:

```
from gpiozero import LED
from time import sleep
class TriLED():
    def __init__(self, pin1=None,pin2=None,pin3=None):
        self.LEDs=(LED(pin1),LED(pin2),LED(pin3))

    def AllOn(self):
        self.LEDs[0].on()
        self.LEDs[1].on()
        self.LEDs[2].on()

    def AllOff(self):
        self.LEDs[0].off()
        self.LEDs[1].off()
        self.LEDs[2].off()
```

A program to make use of the new class would be something like:

```
leds=TriLED(4,17,27)
while True:
    leds.AllOn()
    sleep(0.001)
    leds.AllOff()
    sleep(0.001)
```

Of course, in a real TriLED application you might have methods for set patterns – rotate left, rotate right and so on, but the general idea is the same.

The CompositeDevice

The CompositeDevice class is designed to help with this general pattern of using a tuple of devices. You add the devices in the constructor and you can add them as unnamed members of a tuple or as named attributes. The difference is that named attributes make it easier to access the sub-devices from the outside world. If you specify a device as a positional parameter, then it is added to a tuple. If you specify a device as a named parameter then attributes with the same name are added. The only slight mystery is how do you access the tuple of devices? The answer is that the CompositeDevice class itself behaves like a tuple and you can access its contents in the usual way. It doesn't achieve this by inheritance. Instead it overrides the __getitem__ magic method which is called when you use indexing. For example:

```
compdev=CompositeDevice(LED(pin1),LED(pin2))
compdev[1].on()
```

turns on the LED on pin2.

Named parameters are easier to understand:

```
compdev=CompositeDevice(led1=LED(pin1),led2=LED(pin2))
compdev.led2.on()
```

You should use the first approach for devices that are used internally and the second if you want to allow outside access to the component devices.

Of course, if you are creating a custom class for some device, then a better idea is to inherit from CompositeDevice rather than create an instance so that your custom class inherits the same behavior.

This is easier to understand after an example. The TriLED class can be implemented using CompositeDevice inheritance as:

```
 class TriLED(CompositeDevice):
    def __init__(self, pin1=None,pin2=None,pin3=None):
        super(TriLED,
self).__init__(LED(pin1),LED(pin2),LED(pin3))

    def AllOn(self):
        self[0].on()
        self[1].on()
        self[2].on()

    def AllOff(self):
        self[0].off()
        self[1].off()
        self[2].off()
```

Notice that now it is the instance of TriLED that behaves as a container for the LEDs:

```
leds=TriLED(4,17,27)
while True:
    leds[0].on()
    sleep(0.001)
    leds[0].off()
    sleep(0.001)
```

You can see that there is access to the component LEDs, the LED on pin 4 in this case, and, in general, this is to be discouraged – you should provide methods that do the things the user wants to do without them having to access the component parts. This is an ideal and in some situations direct access to the components might be the only way of getting the job done.

If you do want to encourage access from the outside world then use named parameters:

```
class TriLED(CompositeDevice):
    def __init__(self, pin1=None,pin2=None,pin3=None):
        super(TriLED, self).__init__(left=LED(pin1),
                        middle=LED(pin2),right=LED(pin3))
```

Now you can write the more meaningful:

```
leds=TriLED(4,17,27)
while True:
    leds.left.on()
    sleep(0.001)
    ledsleft.off()
    sleep(0.001)
```

The CompositeDevice class also brings some extras of its own. The main one is value, which returns a named tuple with the current value of each device. For example:

```
leds=TriLED(4,17,27)
print(leds.value)
```

displays:

```
TriLEDValue(device_0=0, device_1=0, device_2=0)
```

For unnamed devices the class assigns a name, while for named devices the name given is used. You can adjust the order in which the devices are listed in the tuple using the _order parameter - the underscore at the start of the name is a sure sign that you are not expected to need it. For example, changing the call to the constructor to:

```
super(TriLED, self).__init__(left=LED(pin1),middle=LED(pin2),
                right=LED(pin3),_order=["right","left","middle"])
```

results in printing:

```
TriLEDValue(right=0, left=0, middle=0)
```

If you need to create an identical type, the namedtuple attribute provides the class of the named tuple used to report the value. This is helpful if you are using the CompositeOutputDevice class.

CompositeOutputDevice

Usually a composite device has both input and output devices, but if it only has output the CompositeOutputDevice adds a few extra methods to CompositeDevice that are useful. In particular:

◆ on() turns all devices on

◆ off() turns all devices off

◆ toggle() turns any on device off and any off device on.

Also the value attribute is modified to allow you to set the state of all of the output devices.

The `CompositeOutputDevice` makes implementing `TriLED` much easier:

```
from gpiozero import LED, CompositeOutputDevice
from time import sleep

class TriLED(CompositeOutputDevice):
    def __init__(self, pin1=None,pin2=None,pin3=None):
        super(TriLED, self).__init__(left=LED(pin1),
                         middle=LED(pin2),right=LED(pin3))
```

Notice that now you don't have to define an `allOn` or `allOff` as they are inherited as `on` and `off`.

In addition you can now set the state of all of the output devices in one operation:

```
leds=TriLED(4,17,27)
while True:
    leds.value=leds.namedtuple(0,1,1)
    sleep(0.001)
    leds.value=leds.namedtuple(1,0,0)
    sleep(0.001)
```

This sets the LED on pin1 low and the other two high and then sets pin 1 high and the other two low.

LEDCollection

Devices with sets of LEDs are so common and so easy to make that there is a special `LEDCollection` version of `CompositeOutputDevice` which creates a tuple of `LED` or `PWMLED` objects. The default is to create `LED` objects, but you can change this using `pwm=True` in the constructor. It inherits the `on`, `off` and `toggle` methods from `CompositeOutputDevice` and has an `leds` attribute which gets or sets the `LED` tuple.

Using this we can implement `TriLED` as:

```
class TriLED(LEDCollection):
    def __init__(self, pin1=None,pin2=None,pin3=None):
        super(TriLED, self).__init__(left=pin1,
                         middle=pin2,right=pin3)
```

Notice that now we don't need to specify that we are creating `LED` objects, just the pins used. Once you have an instance of this new class you can use it as before.

The `LEDCollection` class is used to implement many of the LED classes discussed below.

LED Classes

The simplest of the LED classes is `LEDBoard`:

- ### LEDBoard

    ```
    LEDBoard(*pins, pwm=False, active_high=True,
    initial_value=False, pin_factory=None, **named_pins)
    ```

    This is the simplest of the composite LED devices and is just a collection of LEDs wired to specified GPIO pins, for example:

    ```
    board=LEDBoard(4,17,27)
    ```

    In addition to turning all of the LEDs on or off, and setting them to toggle, blink and pulse, you can control individual LEDs by specifying the device number. For example:

    ```
    board.on(1)
    ```

    turns on just the first specified LED, i.e. the one connected to GPIO4. You can use this in `on`, `off` and `toggle`, but not in `pulse` or `blink`.

- ### LED Character Displays

    Two classes methods, `LEDCharDisplay` and `LEDMultiCharDisplay`, can be used to display information on a multi-segment LED:

    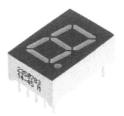

    These have 7, 9, 14 or 16 linear LED segments which can be turned on to form a range of characters:

    ```
               a
            ━━━━━
      f  |\i|j/|  b
         | \|/k|
         g━━ ━━h
      e  | /|\n|  c
         |/l|m\|
            ━━━━━  •  dp
               d
    ```

180

Each of the segments is assigned a letter and each segment is connected to a GPIO line. The constructor is called with the GPIO numbers specified in a to n order.

```
LEDCharDisplay(*pins,dp=pin, font=dict, pwm=False,
    active_high=True, initial_value=" ", pin_factory=None)
```

For example:

```
char = LEDCharDisplay(4, 5, 6, 7, 8, 9, 10,
active_high=False)
```

specifies that a is connected to GPIO4 and b to GPIO5 and so on. You can specify if the segment is on when the line is high or low. To display a character you simply set the value property. For example:

```
char.value=5
```

will display 5 on the display constructed earlier. The way that this works is that the font object defines a mapping from characters to a tuple of segments that should be on to display that character. The pattern is defined by a dict which is indexed by the character and has a tuple defining the state of the segments as a value. For example:

```
myFont=LEDCharFont({"0":(1,1,1,1,1,1,0)}
```

defines a font for the zero character on a seven segment display. The font object is used to set the segments when you assign to value and it is used as a lookup when you read value so the character displayed is returned. Default font objects are provided for 7- and 14-segment displays.

The LEDCharDisplay only handles a single LED display, i.e. one character. If you want a multi-character display then you need to use the LEDMultiCharDisplay class. It is important to realize that multi-character displays vary greatly in their design and pin outs. The type that LEDMultiCharDisplay assumes is just a collection of single LED displays put together with no special drivers. Each separate LED display is fed by the same segment driving GPIO lines. An additional GPIO line is used to strobe each LED digit on and off. By pulsing the strobe lines fast enough and changing the segments synchronously, it looks as if all of the characters are displaying all of the time. Usually you need a transistor driver for each character in this configuration.

To construct an LEDMultiCharDisplay you first create an LEDCharDisplay that represents a single character in the multi-character display. You also specify GPIO lines which switch each character on. For example:

```
char = LEDCharDisplay(4, 5, 6, 7, 8, 9, 10,
                                active_high=False)
d = LEDMultiCharDisplay(c, 19, 20, 21, 22)
```

creates an instance that will control a four-digit display with each digit using GPIO 4, 5, 6, 7, 8, 9, 10 respectively to control what is displayed and GPIO 19 controls the first digit and so on. You set the display using:

```
d.value = "1234"
```

and you can also include a decimal point if the display has one. There is one other property:

```
d.plex_delay = s
```

sets the multiplexing to s seconds. This is the rate that the individual digits are updated and it is usually around 0.005s, i.e. 5ms.

◆ **LEDBarGraph**

This treats the LEDs connected to the specified pins as a bar graph:

```
LEDBarGraph(*pins, pwm=False, active_high=True,
                        initial_value=0, pin_factory=None)
```

Setting a value between -1 and 1 lights up the corresponding proportion of the LEDs with negative values, working from the top of the list of pins. So:

```
graph.value=0.5
```

sets the first half of the LEDs on and:

```
graph.value=-0.5
```

sets the last half of the LEDs on.

It is worth knowing that you can get packaged LED Bars with 10 or 20 segments. However, you need to keep in mind that allocating even as few as 10 GPIO lines to drive such a device might leave you short for other applications.

◆ TrafficLights

```
TrafficLights(red, amber, green, *, yellow=None,
    pwm=False, initial_value=False, pin_factory=None)
```

This controls a simple traffic light device by specifying the pins that the red, amber and green LEDs are connected to. You can control the lights using the red, amber, green attributes. The attribute yellow can be used as an alternative name for amber. You have to provide the code that changes the lights, e.g. green, red/amber, red and so on. You can also use PWM to vary the brightness, but it isn't clear why you might want to do this.

I/O Classes For Other devices

There are also some classes that work with off-the-shelf boards made by a number of different companies.

◆ Energenie

```
Energenie(socket=n, initial_value=False, pin_factory=None)
```

The Energenie socket controller is an easy way of turning mains voltage devices on and off. It makes use of a Pi-mote Hat to connect to an RF controlled socket. It is important to notice that the Energenie system isn't standard and it doesn't work with other smart sockets. The standard methods are off() and on() and you can use the socket property to discover the socket number and value to find the state.

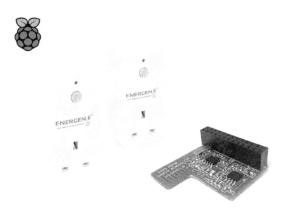

◆ PiHutXmasTree

```
PiHutXmasTree(*, pwm=False, initial_value=False,
                                pin_factory=None)
```

This uses 25 GPIO lines. which are fixed so you don't need to specify them. The 24 LEDs are controlled using attributes `led0` to `led23` and the white LED at the top is the star. You can use PWM to vary the brightness and you can set multiple LEDs in one operation using value.

◆ LedBorg

```
LedBorg(*,pwm=True,initial_value=(0, 0, 0),
                                pin_factory=None)
```

This is a single very bright RGB LED. Again the GPIO lines used are fixed and you can use the `color(R,G,B)` method to set the color. If you use PWM then you can create intermediate colors.

◆ PiLiter

```
PiLiter(*, pwm=False, initial_value=False, pin_factory=None)
```

No longer available.

- **PiLiterBarGraph**

  ```
  PiLiterBarGraph(*, pwm=False, initial_value=False,
                                          pin_factory=None)
  ```

  No longer available.

- **SnowPi**

  ```
  SnowPi(*, pwm=False, initial_value=False, pin_factory=None)
  ```

  No longer available.

- **PiTraffic**

  ```
  PiTraffic(*, pwm=False, initial_value=False,
                                      pin_factory=None)
  ```

  A simple red, amber, green LED board with fixed GPIO lines. Works like `TrafficLights`, but with GPIO9, 10 and 11 fixed.

- **PiStop**

  ```
  PiStop(location, *, pwm=False, initial_value=False,
                                      pin_factory=None)
  ```

  Another traffic light device, but this one is engineered to look like a traffic light and it plugs into one of a set number of locations on the Pi's GPIO connector. You have to specify the location in the constructor A, A+, B, B+, C, D.

◆ **Pibrella**

`PiBrella(pwm=False,pin_factory=None)`

No longer available.

◆ **StatusZero**

`StatusZero(*labels, pwm=False, active_high=True,`
`                    initial_value=False, pin_factory=None)`

This is a traffic light-like device but with three sets of red/green LEDs that can be used to display more general status information beyond stop and start. You can specify labels in the constructor for each of the three indicators, for example:

`status=StatusZero("Temperature", "Humidity")`
`status.Temperature.green.on()`
`status.Humidity.red.on()`

If you don't specify a label then "One", "Two" and "Three" are used. There are three strips next to the LEDs that allow labels to be written using marker pen.

◆ **PumpkinPi**

`PumpkinPi(*,pwm=False,initial_value=False, pin_factory=None)`

This Halloween-specific device has a very specific arrangement of LEDs with methods to control two natural groups, its periphery (sides) and its eyes. The LEDs around the edge of the pumpkin are controlled by `sides` an `LEDBoard` instance. It has attributes `left` and `right` which are also `LEDBoards` for the LEDs on the left and right each of which contains four attributes:

`top, midtop, middle, midbottom, bottom`

The two LEDS representing the Pumpkin's eyes are controlled by `eyes`, an `LEDBoard` that contains:

`left, right`

For example:
```
pPi=PumpkinPi()
pPi.sides.on()
pPi.eyes.left.on()
```
turns on all the LEDs around the Pumpkin's edge and its left eye.

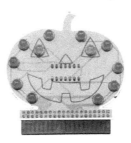

General I/O Composite Classes

There are some general input/output composite devices.

◆ ButtonBoard

```
ButtonBoard(*pins, pull_up=True, active_state=None,
        bounce_time=None, hold_time=1, hold_repeat=False,
                    pin_factory=None, **named_pins)
```

This is the input equivalent of the LEDBoard. A set of buttons, each wired to a different specified pin, can be used as a group. You can read all of the buttons via value, which returns a named tuple of the button states. You can also use values to set a source on an output device:

```
leds.source = btns.values
```

Now any button pressed lights the corresponding LED in the LEDBoard.

You can also use other Button methods - wait_for_press, wait_for_release, is_pressed, pressed_time, when_pressed and when_released, but these work if any button in the group is pressed or released and this is generally not what you want to do. However, you can customize actions depending on which button is pressed by testing within the event handlers. For example:

```
btns.wait_for_press()
state=btns.values
```

lets you test state to see which button is pressed.

◆ TrafficLightsBuzzer

```
TrafficLightsBuzzer(lights, buzzer, button, *,
pin_factory=None)
```

A composite consisting of a `TrafficLights` instance, a `buzzer` and a `button`. You can control the `TrafficLights` using the `lights` attribute, the buzzer via `buzzer` and the button via `button`.

For example:

```
tlb=TrafficLightsBuzzer(TrafficLights(4,17,27), Buzzer(22),
Button(23))
tlb.lights.red.on()
tlb.button.wait_for_press()
tlb.buzzer.on()
tlb.lights.red.off()
tlb.lights.green.on()
tlb.buzzer.off()
```

◆ FishDish

```
FishDish(*, pwm=False, pin_factory=None)
```

This is an off-the-shelf implementation of `TrafficLightsBuzzer` using fixed GPIO pins.

◆ TrafficHat

```
TrafficHat(*, pwm=False, pin_factory=None)
```

Another off-the-shelf implementation of `TrafficLightsBuzzer` using fixed GPIO pins, but no longer available.

◆ **JamHat**

JamHat(*, pwm=False, pin_factory=None)

A composite of 6 LEDs, two red, two yellow and two green, plus two buttons and a tonal buzzer. It uses fixed GPIO lines and the component devices are accessed via attributes:

- lights_1, lights_2

  Two LEDBoard instances representing the top (lights_1) and bottom (lights_2) rows of three LEDs.

- red, yellow, green

  LED or PWMLED instances representing the red, yellow, and green LEDs along the top row.

- button_1, button_2

  The left (button_1) and right (button_2)

- buzzer

189

The Robots

The biggest of the composite classes are the five robots, all of which inherit from `Robot`.

◆ Robot

```
Robot(left=motor, right=motor, *, pwm=True,
                            pin_factory=None)
```

This is a class to control a two-wheeled robot with motors specified. For example:

```
robby=Robot(left=motor(4,17),right=motor(27,22))
```

creates a robot with motors connected to the specified pins via H-bridges – see Chapter 11. You can specify a third enable pin if required. Both motors are PWM speed controlled by default. Access to each of the motors is provided by `left_motor` and `right_motor` and you can use the motors as standard `Motor` objects to control the speed and direction of each wheel.

You can also specify PhaseEnableMotor or a custom motor class.

The `Robot` class also has some methods to do the job directly:

* `backward(speed=1, **kwargs)`
* `forward(speed=1, **kwargs)`

   Drive the robot backward or forward at the set speed.

You can also use two keyword parameters to move along curves:

* `curve_left =c`
* `curve_right=c`

   where c is between 0 (no curve) and 1(maximum curve)

For hard turns we have:

* `left(speed=1)`
* `right(speed=1)`

   Make the robot turn left or right by running one motor forward and the other motor backward.

The final simple methods are:

* `reverse()`

   Reverses each motor's direction.

* `stop()`

   Stops the motors.

PhaseEnableRobot

`PhaseEnableRobot(left, right, *, pwm=True, pin_factory=None)`

This is very similar to the `Robot` class, but the `left` and `right` tuples specify the phase, forward, back, and speed. It is now deprecated in favor of Robot defined with a PhaseEnableMotor.

CamJamKitRobot

`CamJamKitRobot(*, pwm=True, pin_factory=None)`

A basic `Robot` derived class with fixed pin assignments. The kit includes ultrasonic sensors and a line follower which aren't handled in the `CamJamKitRobot` class. You have to 3D-print your own chassis. It has all of the motor control methods of the Robot class.

PololuDRV8835Robot

`PololuDRV8835Robot(*, pwm=True, pin_factory=None)`

This really isn't a complete robot, just a motor controller which uses phase, forward, back, and speed. If you connect two motors to it then you have all of the methods provided by the Robot class.

RyanteckRobot

`RyanteckRobot(*, pwm=True, pin_factory=None)`
No longer available

Refactoring the Stepper Motor Class

When creating custom classes the first step is to get something working. This is usually rough and ready and really just a proof that things work as you think they do. The next step is to polish your creation. In object-oriented programming this is often referred to as "refactoring" and it often involves removing code from one class and using it to implement a new class. In the case of the stepper motor class we created in Chapter 11, we didn't make use of CompositeDevice to contain the component parts of the device. This is easy to put right:

```
from gpiozero import DigitalOutputDevice,CompositeDevice

class StepperBi4(CompositeDevice):
    def __init__(self, A=None,Am=None,B=None,Bm=None):
        if not all(p is not None for p in [A,Am,B,Bm]):
            raise GPIOPinMissing(
                'Four GPIO pins must be provided'
            )
        super(StepperUni4, self).__init__(DigitalOutputDevice(A),
                DigitalOutputDevice(B),DigitalOutputDevice(Am),
                    DigitalOutputDevice(Bm))
        self.phase=0
        self.halfstepSeq = [
                            [1,0,0,0],
                            [1,1,0,0],
                            [0,1,0,0],
                            [0,1,1,0],
                            [0,0,1,0],
                            [0,0,1,1],
                            [0,0,0,1],
                            [1,0,0,1]
                           ]

    def setPhase(self,phase):
        self.phase=phase
        for gpio,state in zip(self, self.halfstepSeq[phase]):
            gpio.pin._set_state(state)

    def stepForward(self):
        self.phase=(self.phase+1) % 8
        self.setPhase(self.phase)

    def stepReverse(self):
        self.phase=(self.phase-1) % 8
        self.setPhase(self.phase)
```

The only real difference is that now we are using CompositeDevice to store the DigitalOutputDevice objects within a tuple. As already explained, the inheriting class acts as the container. So we now refer to each `DigitalOutputDevice` as `self(0)`, `self(1)` and so on with `self` being the complete tuple of devices.

Once we have an instance the same idea works, so:

```
step=StepperBi4(4,17,27,22)
step(0).on()
```

turns on the first `CompositeDevice`, i.e. phase A. The stepper motor class is used in the same way as before:

```
step=StepperBi4(4,17,27,22)
step.setPhase(0)
while True:
    sleep(0.001)
    step.stepForward()
```

Background Stepper

One final improvement that is worth making to the `StepperBi4` device is allowing it to be used in continuous rotation mode without having to use the main program to perform each step. The idea is to create an additional thread that implements the stepping and integrate this into GPIO Zero. This is slightly advanced so if you don't want to know about how to use GPIO Zero threading skip this section.

We need a rotation method that can be run in another thread:

```
def _rotate(self, dir, speed):
    delay = 60/(speed*400)-0.001
    while True:
        if dir == 1:
            self.stepForward()
        if dir == -1:
            self.stepReverse()
        if self._rotate_thread.stopping.wait(delay):
            break
```

The only part of the method that you might not be familiar with is the `wait` method. GPIO Zero implements its own version of the thread object complete with a `stopping` event object which is used to signal that the thread is coming to an end. In this case the event object's `wait` method is use to provide a pause for `delay` seconds. If the thread is being stopped then the `if` statement executes the break. Notice that the `stepForward` and `stepReverse` are the standard methods given earlier.

We also need a method to stop the thread:

```
def _stop_rotate(self):
    if getattr(self, '_rotate_thread', None):
        self._rotate_thread.stop()
        self._rotate_thread = None
```

And finally a method to start the thread to run the rotate method for the forward and reverse directions:

```
    def forward(self,speed=0):
        self._stop_rotate()
        if speed==0: return
        self._rotate_thread = GPIOThread(target=self._rotate,
                                              args=(+1,speed))
        self._rotate_thread.start()
    def reverse(self,speed=1):
        self._stop_rotate()
        if speed==0: return
        self._rotate_thread = GPIOThread(target=self._rotate,
                                              args=(-1,speed))
        self._rotate_thread.start()
```

You can see that in each case first any thread that was already running is stopped and a new thread is created using GPIO Zero's GPIOThread class. The target parameter sets the method to run, i.e. _rotate, and passes it the arguments specified. Finally the thread is started.

The complete program is:

```
from gpiozero import DigitalOutputDevice,CompositeDevice
from time import sleep
from gpiozero.threads import GPIOThread
class StepperBi4(CompositeDevice):
    def __init__(self, A=None,Am=None,B=None,Bm=None):
        if not all(p is not None for p in [A,Am,B,Bm]):
            raise GPIOPinMissing('Four GPIO pins must be provided')
        super(StepperUni4, self).__init__(DigitalOutputDevice(A),
                DigitalOutputDevice(B),DigitalOutputDevice(Am),
                    DigitalOutputDevice(Bm))
        self.phase=0
        self._rotate_thread=None
        self.halfstepSeq = [
                            [1,0,0,0],
                            [1,1,0,0],
                            [0,1,0,0],
                            [0,1,1,0],
                            [0,0,1,0],
                            [0,0,1,1],
                            [0,0,0,1],
                            [1,0,0,1]
                           ]
```

```
    def setPhase(self,phase):
        self.phase=phase
        for gpio,state in zip(self, self.halfstepSeq[phase]):
            gpio.pin._set_state(state)

    def stepForward(self):
        self.phase=(self.phase+1) % 8
        self.setPhase(self.phase)

    def stepReverse(self):
        self.phase=(self.phase-1) % 8
        self.setPhase(self.phase)

    def forward(self,speed=0):
        self._stop_rotate()
        if speed==0: return
        self._rotate_thread = GPIOThread(target=self._rotate,
                                                 args=(+1,speed))
        self._rotate_thread.start()

    def reverse(self,speed=1):
        self._stop_rotate()
        if speed==0: return
        self._rotate_thread = GPIOThread(target=self._rotate,
                                                 args=(-1,speed))
        self._rotate_thread.start()

    def _rotate(self,dir,speed):
        delay=60/(speed*400)-0.001
        while True:
            if dir==1:
                self.stepForward()
            if dir==-1:
                self.stepReverse()
            if self._rotate_thread.stopping.wait(delay):
                break
    def _stop_rotate(self):
        if getattr(self, '_rotate_thread', None):
            self._rotate_thread.stop()
        self._rotate_thread = None
```
With this modification, we can now run the motor forward or reverse at a specified speed without the main program being involved. For example:
```
step=StepperBi4(4,17,27,22)
step.setPhase(0)
while True:
    step.forward(60)
    sleep(1)
    step.reverse(30)
    sleep(1)
```

Summary

- Inheritance isn't the only way classes can be reused. Composition, or containment, i.e. placing instances of other classes in a class, is also very useful.

- The CompositeDevice class makes creating compound devices very easy and more organized than an ad hoc approach.

- The CompositeOutputDevice class adds some methods that are appropriate for a compound device that contains nothing but output devices.

- Driving multiple LEDs is so common a task that there is a special class, LEDCollection, designed to do just this.

- There are a large number of off-the-shelf compound devices based on LEDCollection. Even though they are proprietary devices, it is easy to make your own from basic components.

- There are also some more general, off-the-shelf, compound devices that use LED, Buttons and sound devices.

- There are a set of robot classes which essentially consist of motor objects and methods to allow control in terms of direction and speed.

- The stepper motor class created in earlier chapters is easy to refactor using CompositeDevice and you can even add a background task to make it rotate without the involvement of the main program.

The Pi offers three standard protocols for connecting more sophisticated devices – serial or RS232, Serial Peripheral Interface or SPI, and I2C. Of these, GPIO Zero supports only the SPI bus and this is the one we need to look at first.

As long as you restrict your attention to the devices that GPIO Zero supports, then everything is very easy. The good news is that if you are prepared to spend a little time understanding how the SPI bus works, you can easily add your own custom devices. If you want to use the I2C, or any other bus, then you need to look beyond GPIO Zero. You could move to C and interface directly with the hardware or, if you want to stay with Python, you could use Linux drivers, in which case see *Raspberry Pi IOT in Python with Linux Drivers, 2nd Ed*, ISBN:9781871962864.

SPI Bus Basics

In the configuration most used for the Pi, there is a single master and, at most, two slaves.

The signal lines are:

- ◆ MOSI (Master Output Slave Input), i.e. data to the slave
- ◆ MISO (Master Input Slave Output), i.e. data to the master
- ◆ SCLK (Serial Clock), which is always generated by the master

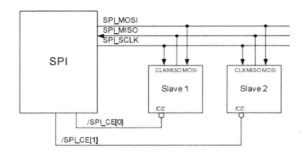

In general, there can also be any number of SS (Slave Select) or CE (Chip Enable) lines, which are usually set low to specify which slave is being addressed. Notice that unlike other buses, I2C for example, there are no SPI standard commands or addresses, only bytes of data. However, slave devices do interpret some of the data as commands to do something or send some particular data.

The pins that are used for the Pi's SPI0 bus are:

SPI0		
Function	**Pin**	**GPIO Line**
MOSI	19	GPIO10
MISO	21	GPIO09
SCLK	23	GPIO11
CE0	24	GPIO08
CE1	26	GPIO07

GPIO Zero supports the SPI0 bus, but only via the Linux SPI driver `spidev` and the Python `spidev` library, which should already be installed. However, to make use of the SPI driver you have to enable it. You can do this either by using `raspi-config`, or by ensuring the line `dtparam=spi=on` isn't commented out in `/boot/config.txt`, and rebooting. If the SPI driver is loaded, you should see the file `/dev/spidev0.0`.

If you want to activate the driver in Python code then use:

```
import subprocess
temp = subprocess.Popen(["sudo", "dtparam", "-l"],
                                stdout = subprocess.PIPE)
output = str(temp.communicate())
print(output)
lastSPI=output.rfind("spi")
```

```
if lastSPI!=-1:
    lastSPI=output.find("spi=on",lastSPI)
    if lastSPI==-1:
        temp = subprocess.Popen(["sudo", "dtparam", "spi=on"],
                                     stdout = subprocess.PIPE)
        output = str(temp.communicate())
        print("adding",output)
else:
    temp = subprocess.Popen(["sudo", "dtparam", "spi=on"],
                                 stdout = subprocess.PIPE)
    output = str(temp.communicate())
    print("adding",output)
```

This works by first using the `dtparam -l` command to list the loaded overlays. If the `spi` overlay is already loaded nothing is done. If it isn't then it runs the command `dtparam spi=on`. You can also remove overlays in the same way, but this isn't a good idea as things tend to be unstable if you do. Better to leave the overlay loaded and wait for the next reboot to remove it.

There is a software-emulated SPI mode in GPIO Zero, but it is slow and doesn't always work. This doesn't depend on the Linux driver, however, and can be used without turning the driver on. There is more about this at the end of the chapter.

The SPI Devices

GPIO Zero supports a set of SPI devices at a very high level. There are objects that implement the custom interface that these devices use. If you only need to use one of these then GPIO Zero SPI is trivial.

Unfortunately, all of the supported SPI devices are A to D converters:

◆ MCP3001

10-bit analog to digital converter with 1 differential channel.

◆ MCP3002

10-bit analog to digital converter with 2 channels (0-1) with optional differential mode.

◆ MCP3004

10-bit analog to digital converter with 4 channels (0-3) with optional differential mode.

- ◆ MCP3008

  10-bit analog to digital converter with 8 channels (0-7) with optional differential mode.

- ◆ MCP3201

  12-bit analog to digital converter with 1 differential channel.

- ◆ MCP3202

  12-bit analog to digital converter with 2 channels (0-1) with optional differential mode.

- ◆ MCP3204

  12-bit analog to digital converter with 4 channels (0-3) with optional differential mode.

- ◆ MCP3208

  12-bit analog to digital converter with 8 channels (0-7) with optional differential mode.

- ◆ MCP3301

  Signed 13-bit analog to digital converter with a single differential channel

- ◆ MCP3302

  12/13-bit analog to digital converter with 4 channels (0-3). When operated in differential mode, the device outputs a signed 13-bit value which is scaled from -1 to +1. When operated in single-ended mode (the default), the device outputs an unsigned 12-bit value scaled from 0 to 1.

- ◆ MCP3304

  12/13-bit analog to digital converter with 8 channels (0-7). When operated in differential mode, the device outputs a signed 13-bit value which is scaled from -1 to +1. When operated in single-ended mode (the default), the device outputs an unsigned 12-bit value scaled from 0 to 1.

All of these devices work in more or less the same way and to demonstrate how to use them let's connect up an 8-channel, 12-bit A to D converter using the MCP3008. This is often sufficient for many projects.

The MCP3008

The MCP3008 is available in a number of different packages, but the standard 16-pin PDIP is the easiest to work with using a prototyping board. You can buy it from the usual sources, including Amazon if you need one in a hurry.

Its pinouts are fairly self-explanatory:

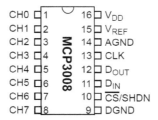

You can see that the analog inputs are on the left and the power and SPI bus connections are on the right. The conversion accuracy is claimed to be 10 bits, but how many of these bits correspond to reality and how many are noise depends on how you design the layout of the circuit.

You need to take great care if you need high accuracy. For example, you will notice that there are two voltage inputs V_{DD} and V_{REF}. V_{DD} is the supply voltage that runs the chip and V_{REF} is the reference voltage that is used to compare the input voltage. Obviously, if you want highest accuracy, V_{REF}, which has to be lower than or equal to V_{DD}, should be set by an accurate low-noise voltage source. However, in most applications V_{REF} and V_{DD} are simply connected together and the usual, low- quality, supply voltage is used as the reference. If this isn't good enough then you can use anything from a Zener diode to a precision voltage reference chip, such as the TL431. At the very least, however, you should add a $1\mu F$ capacitor connected to the V_{DD} pin and the V_{REF} pin to ground.

The MC3000 family is a type of A to D called a successive approximation converter. You don't need to know how it works to use it, but it isn't difficult to understand. The idea is that first a voltage equal to $V_{REF}/2$ is generated and the input voltage is compared to this. If it is lower then the most significant bit is a 0 and if it is greater than or equal then it is a 1. At the next step the voltage generated is $V_{REF}/2+V_{REF}/4$ and the comparison is repeated to generate the next bit.

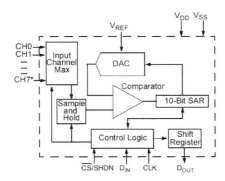

You can see that successive approximation fits in well with a serial bus as each bit can be obtained in the time needed to transmit the previous bit. However, the conversion is relatively slow and a sample-and-hold circuit has to be used to keep the input to the converter stage fixed. The sample and hold takes the form of a 20pF capacitor and a switch. The only reason you need to know about this is that the conversion has to be completed in a time that is short compared to the discharge time of the capacitor. So, for accuracy, there is a minimum SPI clock rate as well as a maximum.

Also, to charge the capacitor quickly enough for it to follow a changing voltage, it needs to be connected to a low-impedance source. In most cases this isn't a problem, but if it is you need to include an op amp.

If you are using an op amp buffer then you might as well implement an anti-aliasing filter to remove frequencies from the signal that are too fast for the A to D to respond to. How all this works would take us into the realm of analog electronics and signal processing and well beyond the core subject matter of this book.

You can also use the A to D channels in pairs, i.e. in differential mode, to measure the voltage difference between them. For example, in differential mode you measure the difference between CH0 and CH1, i.e. what you measure is CH1-CH0. In most cases you want to use all eight channels in single-ended mode. In principle, you can take 200k samples per second, but only at the upper limit of the supply voltage, i.e. V_{DD}=5V, falling to 75k samples per second at its lower limit of V_{DD}=2.7V.

The SPI clock limits are a maximum of 3.6MHz at 5V and 1.35MHz at 2.7V. The clock can go slower, but because of the problem with the sample and hold mentioned earlier, it shouldn't go below 10kHz.

How fast we can take samples is discussed later in this chapter.

Connecting the MCP3008 to the Pi

The connection to the Pi's SPI bus is very simple and can be seen in the diagram below.

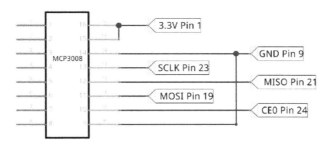

The only additional component that is recommended is a $1\mu F$ capacitor connected, between pins 15 and 16, to ground, mounted as close to the chip as possible. As discussed in the previous section, you might want a separate voltage reference for pin 15, rather than just using the 3.3V supply.

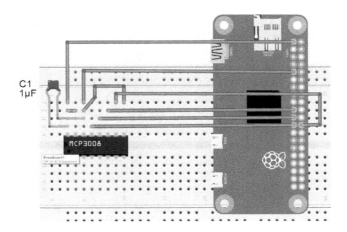

The program that reads the voltage on any of the device's pins is exceptionally simple:

```
from gpiozero import MCP3008

adc=MCP3008(channel=0)
print(adc.value)
```

The MCP3008 class returns an object that can be used to read the A to D converter's channel by calling its value method. Each time you call value, a new conversion is initiated. If this program doesn't work and you get a

203

warning message, then it is almost certain that you don't have the Linux driver installed. If you look beyond the warning message, you should see that the program has worked. The reason is that, if the Linux driver isn't found, GPIO Zero falls back to a software implementation, which is slow but works in this case. If the program works, but you get silly readings then it is almost certain that you have wired the circuit incorrectly or have a malfunctioning component.

It is assumed that the reference voltage is 3.3V and the value returned is scaled to the range 0.0 to 1.0. You can set the reference voltage using:

```
max_voltage=Vref
```

If you want to work in differential mode you have to add:

```
differential=True
```

That's all there is to it. You can specify which SPI interface to use, but as only one is supported this is redundant.

The Software Fallback

If you want to use the software implementation you can specify the GPIO pins used for each SPI function. For example, the previous A to D program can be written:

```
adc=MCP3008(channel=0, clock_pin=11, mosi_pin=10,
                                miso_pin=9, select_pin=8)
print(adc.value)
```

Notice that now we are specifying the GPIO lines to be used for each SPI function. In this case these are the same as the hardware-provided SPI pins, but if the Linux driver isn't loaded the software implementation is used. Of course, if you select a set of pins that aren't supported by the Linux driver, then the software implementation is always used. You can silence the warning that the software implementation is about to be used with:

```
import warnings
warnings.simplefilter('ignore')
```

How Fast?

How fast the SPI interface can work is a complicated question. A simpler one is how fast does the default hardware SPI interface work when reading an A to D? The program to find this out is:

```
from gpiozero import MCP3008
adc=MCP3008(channel=0)
while True:
    adc.value
```

The result can be found using a logic analyzer to measure the time between readings as indicated by the CS0 line, see later for more on the SPI protocol:

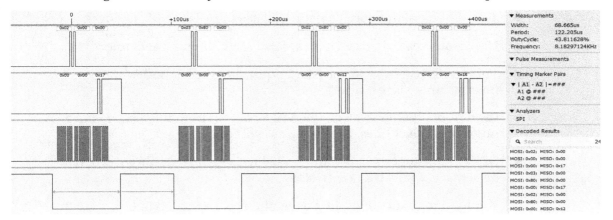

You can see that the repeat rate is 8.28kHz on a Pi 4, with a similar figure on the Pi Zero. If you try the same thing out using the software interface then the repeat rate drops to 1.8kHz, nearly five times slower. The software interface works well as long as you don't need speed. Compare this to the rate of 36kHz that can be achieved using direct C programming. Notice also that these figures are for just reading the A to D - no processing was performed which would slow the process down. These are the upper limits on what you can achieve with the default, software SPI interfaces.

Summary

- The SPI bus is often problematic because there is no SPI standard.

- Unlike other serial buses, it makes use of unidirectional connections.

- The data lines are MOSI (master output slave input) and MISO (master input slave output).

- In addition, there is a clock line SCLK, output from the master, and a number of select lines, two in the case of the Pi.

- GPIO Zero supports hardware-SPI using the Linux driver on SPI0 or on any set of pins using software.

- You have to enable the driver using the `dtparam` command.

- The MCP3000 range of A to D converters is very easy to use via GPIO Zero SPI. All you have to do is create an instance of the appropriate MCP3000 class and then use the `value` property to read the voltage.

- You can read data at rates as fast as 8kHz, which isn't fast enough for audio applications.

Chapter 14

Custom SPI Devices

If you only want to use SPI A to D converter chips, you already know enough about SPI. However, the SPI bus is commonly encountered as it is used to connect all sorts of devices, from LCD displays to real time clocks, and not just A to D converters. If you want to write your own code to work with other devices then GPIO Zero makes this relatively easy, but you do need to know a little more about how SPI works.

SPI Software

The SPI bus is odd - it does not use bidirectional serial connections. There is a data line for the data to go from the master to the slave and a separate data line from the slave back to the master. That is, instead of a single data line that changes its transfer direction, there is one for data out and one for data in. It is also worth knowing that the drive on the SPI bus is push-pull, and not open collector/drain. This provides higher speed and more noise protection as the bus is driven in both directions.

Data transfer on the SPI bus is also slightly odd. What happens is that the master pulls one of the chip selects low, which activates a slave. Then the master toggles the clock SCLK and both the master and the slave send a single bit on their respective data lines. After eight clock pulses, a byte has been transferred from the master to the slave and from the slave to the master. You can think of this as being implemented as a circular buffer, although it doesn't have to be.

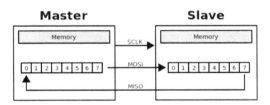

This full-duplex data transfer is often hidden by the software and the protocol used. For example, there is a read function that reads data from the slave and sends zeros or data that is ignored by the slave. Similarly, there is a write function that sends valid data, but ignores whatever the slave sends.

207

The transfer is typically in groups of eight bits, usually most significant bit first, but this isn't always the case. In general, as long as the master supplies clock pulses, data is transferred.

Notice this circular buffer arrangement allows for slaves to be daisy-chained with the output of one going to the input of the next. This makes the entire chain one big circular shift register. This can make it possible to have multiple devices with only a single chip select, but it also means any commands sent to the slaves are received by each one in turn. For example, you could send a convert command to each A to D converter in turn and receive back results from each one.

SPI Device - The Data Transfer Functions

The A to D converter objects all inherit from the SPI class, which is the base class for working with any SPI device. You create an SPI device in the usual way, specifying the SPI port or the GPIO lines to be used. If the device can open the Linux driver on those lines then this is used, otherwise the software interface is used. You have to remember to close the SPI device to release the GPIO lines, otherwise Linux will be unable to manage them.

The SPI Device has a number of methods, provided via the _spi field, that allow you to transfer data and the most fundamental is the transfer function. The _spi field is an instance of the SPI interface class that the pin factory provides. That is, assuming Dev is an instance of SPI Device:

```
wordsIn=Dev._spi._transfer(wordsOut)
```

sends the bytes specified in wordsOut and receives the bytes sent by the client device in wordsIn. The wordsIn and wordsOut variables are simply a list of bytes. So for example:

```
wordsIn=Dev._spi._transfer([0xAA,0xEE])
```

sends two bytes, 0xAA and 0xEE. The returned data is similarly a list of bytes.

There are two functions provided to make the conversion of integers to lists of bytes and vice versa easy:

```
words=Dev._int_to_words(value)
value=Dev._words_to_int(words)
```

The first takes a numeric value and converts it to a list of bytes and the second does the opposite. To see how these work you have to keep in mind that in Python an integer can be as big as you like without loss of precision. For example:

```
words=Dev._int_to_words(0xAABBCCDDEEFF)
print(hex(Dev._words_to_int(words)))
```

prints:
```
0xaabbccddeeff
```

Working in hex isn't essential, but it is often easier as this is how values are specified in data sheets. It is also worth knowing that all of these functions will work with a specified number of bits per byte and this is specified in the SPI interface. It is usually 8 bits.

While transfer is the fundamental data transfer function, most SPI interface classes also provide:

```
words=Dev._spi.read(n)
Dev._spi.write(words)
```

The read function will read n words of data and the write will write the list of words provided and return the number successfully written. They are both generally defined in terms of the transfer function:

```
Dev._spi.read(n)   = Dev._spi.transfer([0]*n)
Dev._spi.write(words)=  return len(Dev._spi.transfer(words))
```

Now we come to a subtle point. What is the difference between transferring multiple bytes in a single transfer call, and simply sending the bytes individually using multiple transfer calls, one per word? The answer is that each time you make a transfer call the chip select line is activated, the data transferred and then it is deactivated. Using a single transfer call to send multiple bytes, the chip select is left active for the entire transfer, i.e. it isn't deactivated between each byte. Sometimes this difference isn't important and you can transfer three bytes using three calls to transfer or by using a single call to transfer. However, some slaves will abort the current multibyte operation if the chip select line is deactivated in the middle of a multibyte transfer.

It is important to realize that the nature of the transfer is that the first byte is sent at the same time that the first byte is received. That is, unlike other protocols, the whole of the send buffer isn't sent before the received data comes back. The whole transfer works a byte at a time – the first byte is sent while the first byte is being received, then the second byte is sent at the same time as the second byte is being received and so on. Not fully understanding this idea can lead to some interesting bugs.

A Loopback Example

Because of the way that data is transferred on the SPI bus, it is very easy to test that everything is working without having to add any components. All you have to do is connect MOSI to MISO so that anything sent is also received in a loopback mode. First connect pin 19 to pin 20 using a jumper wire and start a new project. The program is very simple. As this is a loopback test we really don't need to configure the interface as, however it is configured, it will use the same parameters for input as output.

Create an instance of the SPI Device:

```
Dev=SPIDevice()
```

Next send some data and receive it right back:

```
words=Dev._spi.transfer([0xAA])
```

The hex value AA is useful in testing because it generates the bit sequence 10101010, which is easy to see on a logic analyzer.

Check that the received data matches the sent data:

```
if words[0]==0xAA:
    print("data received correctly")
```

Finally, close the SPI Device:

```
Dev.close()
```

Putting all of this together gives us the complete program:

```
from gpiozero import SPIDevice

Dev=SPIDevice()
words=Dev._spi.transfer([0xAA])
if words[0]==0xAA:
    print("data received correctly")
Dev.close()
```

If you run the program and don't get the "data received correctly" message then the most likely reason is that you have connected the wrong two pins together or not connected them at all.

Configuring the SPI

There are a set of properties that allow you to configure the SPI interface. The reason you need to know how to change the default configuration is that not all SPI devices conform to the default.

There are four modes which define the relationship between the data timing and the clock pulse. The clock can be either active high or low, which is referred to as clock polarity (CPOL) and data can be sampled on the rising or falling edge of the clock, which is clock phase (CPHA).

All combinations of these two possibilities gives the four modes:

SPI Mode*	Clock Polarity CPOL	Clock Edge CPHA	Characteristics
0	0	0	Clock active high data output on falling edge and sampled on rising
1	0	1	Clock active high data output on rising edge and sampled on falling
2	1	0	Clock active low data output on falling edge and sampled on rising
3	1	1	Clock active low data output on rising edge and sampled on falling

*The way that the SPI modes are labeled is common but not universal.

There is often a problem trying to work out what mode a slave device uses. The clock polarity is usually easy and the clock phase can sometimes be worked out from the data transfer timing diagrams and:

- First clock transition in the middle of a data bit means CPHA=0
- First clock transition at the start of a data bit means CPHA=1

You can set the clock mode using:

```
clock_polarity=True or False
clock_phase=True or False
```

or you can set both using

```
clock_mode= 0, 1, 2 or 3
```

You can also set:

```
lsb_first=True or False
```

but the Pi's SPI hardware ignores this.

To set the sense of the chip select to high or low to select, use:

```
select_high=True or False
```

Finally, you can set:

```
bits_per_word=n
```

but again the Pi's SPI hardware defaults to 8 and cannot be changed.

There is one last configuration option which is well hidden and only available on the hardware SPI interface:

```
_interface.maxspeed_hz=f
```

where f is the frequency in Hertz. The default is 500000, i.e. 500kHz, and you can set it to higher frequencies, but these are not guaranteed. On a Pi 4 you can get up to 8MHz, but this doesn't mean that the device connected to the bus will work at this speed.

Loopback Revisited

Now that we know how the SPI interface works and how to configure it, we can return to the loopback example, include configuration and examine its output.

Configuring the SPI interface to clock mode 0, select active low and a clock of 7kHz:

```
from gpiozero import SPIDevice

Dev=SPIDevice()

Dev.clock_mode=0
Dev.select_high=False
Dev._spi._interface.max_speed_hz=7000

words=Dev._spi.transfer([0xAA])
if words[0]==0xAA:
    print("data received correctly")
```

If you connect a logic analyzer to the four pins involved – 19, 21, 23 and 24 - you will see the data transfer:

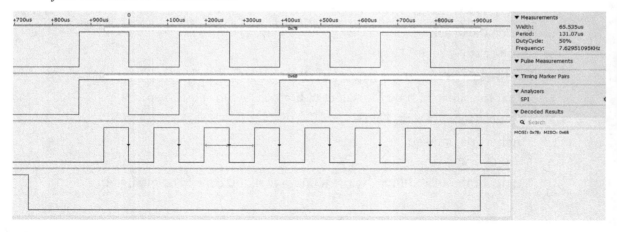

If you look carefully, you will see the CS0 line go low before the master places the first data bit on the MOSI and hence on the MISO lines. The documentation states that the CS line is held for at least three core clock cycles before transfer starts and held for at least one clock cycle when the transfer is complete. Notice that the clock rises in the middle of each data bit, making this a mode 0 transfer. You can also see that the clock is measured to be 7.6kHz on a Pi 4, which is the closest supported frequency to 7kHz.

Implementing the MCP3008

As an example we can re-implement the MCP3008 SPI interface from first principles. The clock rate needs to be reasonably fast, but not so fast that the data starts to corrupt. A clock rate of 60kHz seems reasonable. From the data sheet, the chip select has to be active low and data is sent most significant bit first by default for both the master and the slave. The only puzzle is what mode to use? This is listed in the data sheet and it can be mode 0 with clock active high or mode 3 with clock active low.

We now have enough information to initialize the slave:

```
Dev=SPIDevice()

Dev.clock_mode= 0
Dev.select_high=False
Dev._spi._interface.max_speed_hz=60000
```

Now we have the SPI initialized and ready to transfer data, but what data do we transfer? The SPI bus doesn't have any standard commands or addressing structure. Each device responds to data sent in different ways and sends data back in different ways. You simply have to read the data sheet to find out what the commands and responses are.

Reading the data sheet might be initially confusing because it says that what you have to do is send five bits to the slave - a start bit; a bit that selects its operating mode to single or differential; and a 3-bit channel number. The operating mode is 1 for single-ended and 0 for differential.

So to read Channel 3, i.e. 011, in single-ended mode you would send the slave:

```
11011xxx
```

where xxx means don't care. The response from the slave is that it holds its output in a high impedance state until the sixth clock pulse. It then sends a zero bit on the seventh followed by bit 9 of the data on clock eight.

That is, the slave sends back:

```
xxxxx0b9
```

where x means indeterminate. The remaining 9 bits are sent back in response to the next nine clock pulses. This means you have to transfer three bytes to get all ten bits of data. This all makes reading the data in 8-bit chunks confusing.

The data sheet suggests a different way of doing the job that delivers the data more neatly packed into three bytes. It suggests sending a single byte:

```
00000001
```

The slave transfers random data at the same time, which is ignored. The final 1 is treated as the start bit. If you now transfer a second byte, with most significant bit indicating single or differential mode, then a 3-bit channel address and the remaining bits set to 0, the slave will respond with the null and the top two bits of the conversion. Now all you have to do to get the final eight bits of data is to read a third byte:

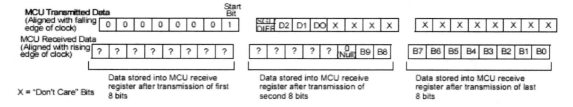

This way you get two neat bytes containing the data with all the low order bits in their correct positions.

Using this information we can now write some instructions that read a given channel. For example, to read Channel 0 we first send a byte set to 0x01 as the start bit and ignore the byte the slave transfers. Next we send 0x80 to select single-ended and channel zero and keep the byte the slave sends back as the high order two bits. Finally, we send a zero byte so that we get the low order bits from the slave:

```
words=Dev._spi.transfer([0x01, 0x80, 0x00])
```

Notice you cannot send the three bytes one at a time using transfer because that results in the CS line being deactivated between the transfer of each byte.

To get the data out of the words list we need to do some bit manipulation:

```
data =   (words[1] & 0x03) << 8 |   words[2];
```

The first part of the expression extracts the low three bits from the first byte the slave sent and as these are the most significant bits they are shifted up eight places. The rest of the bits are then ORed with them to give the full 10-bit result. To convert to volts we use:

```
volts =   data * 3.3 / 1023.0
```

assuming that VREF is 3.3V.

If you connect a logic analyzer to the SPI bus you will see something like:

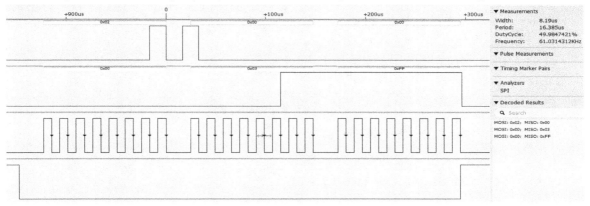

You can see the commands and the response, this case a reading of 3.3V.

The complete program is:

```
from gpiozero import SPIDevice
Dev=SPIDevice()
Dev.clock_mode= 0
Dev.select_high=False
Dev._spi._interface.max_speed_hz=60000

words=Dev._spi.transfer([0x01, 0x80, 0x00])
data =  (words[1] & 0x03) << 8 |  words[2];
volts =  data * 3.3 / 1023.0
print(volts)
Dev.close()
```

A Custom SPI Device – DS3234 Clock

Implementing the MCP3008 is instructive but, given there is already a class that will do the job, not particularly useful. Writing a class for a new SPI device is instructive and practical. The DS3234 RTC (Real Time Clock) is accurate and includes a battery backup that can keep it running for years. It is available from a number of sources in slightly different forms:

215

They share the same pinouts:

Label	Description
GND	Ground (0V) supply
VCC	DS3234 VCC (3.3V) power supply input
SQW	Configurable square-wave output Alarm 1 and/or Alarm 2 interrupt output
CLK	SPI clock input
MISO	SPI master in, slave out
MOSI	SPI master out, slave in
SS	SPI active-low chip select CS0

You will recognize these as the standard SPI interface pins with the addition of SQW. This can be used to generate a square wave signal at a set frequency from 1Hz to 192kHz or it can be used as outputs of either of the two alarm timers. In this example we won't use SQW and it can be left unconnected.

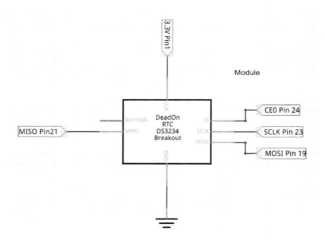

Once you have this connected, you can start to write the software. Notice that you don't need to use a backup battery, but if you don't then the device will lose its time setting each time you switch it off. With a battery it will keep time for years.

To find out how to talk to the device, we need to consult its datasheet. This lists all of the registers that you can read and write and there are quite a few and it all looks complicated. If we are only interested in the date and time, then only the first seven are relevant:

Address read/write		MSB bit7	Bit 6	Bit 5	Bit 4	Bit 3	Bit 2	Bit 1	LSB Bit 0	Function	Range
0x00	0x80	0	Seconds x 10			Seconds				Seconds	00-59
0x01	0x81	0	Minutes x 10			Minutes				Minutes	00-59
0x02	0x82	0	12/24	AM/PM or Hours x10	Hours x10	Hours				Hours	1-12 +AM /PM 00-23
0x03	0x83	0	0	0	0	0	Day			Day	1-7
0x04	0x84	0		Date x 10		Date				Date	01-31
0x05	0x85	Century	0	0	Month x 10	Month				Month	01-12
0x06	0x86	0	Year x10			Year				Year	00-99

You can see that the addresses are sequential - 0x00 to 0x06 for reading and 0x80 to 0x86 for writing. The data is packed into each byte using BCD, Binary Coded Decimal. This codes each decimal digit as a four-bit binary value. For example, the month 12 would be coded in BCD as 0001 and 0010, i.e. 1 and 2 in binary. The value 59 would be coded as 0101 for 5 and 1001 for 9. In a simple system, a single byte would always hold two BCD digits. However, if the range of possible values is limited, some bits are always zero and can be reused for something else. For example, the month register only has to store from 01 to 12 and this means we only need one bit for the tens digit and four for the units digit – and you can see that this is the case in the table. This allows us to use bit 7 as a century indicator. The way this works can be confusing as in some implementations bit 7 == 0, meaning 1900, and in others bit 7 ==1 meaning 2000. This isn't necessary as all the century bit does is increment when a century boundary is crossed. What this means is that we can leave it at 0, to mean 2000, and wait for it to increment to indicate that we have reached 2100.

The only slightly complicated part is specifying the use of a 12- or 24-hour clock in the Hours register. If you set the bit 6 to a 1 then you are selecting a 12-hour clock and you only need five bits to represent the number, i.e. from 0 0000 for 0 hours to 1 0010 for 12 hours. This lets you use bit 5 as an AM/PM indicator. On the other hand, if you set bit 6 to 0 then you need an extra bit because now hours range from 00 0000 for 0 hours to 10 0100 for 24 hours. The simplest thing to do is work with a 24-hour clock then you can simply read the register as a simple BCD coding of the two digits that give the hour.

217

We are almost ready to start coding. The only additional information we need is what clock mode to use. This is surprisingly difficult to discover from the datasheet and you have to look at the timing diagrams to work it out. It turns out that the device will work in mode 1 or mode 3. It is also worth knowing that if you get this wrong, the device will not respond and it will look as if you have a dead component.

The Software

When implementing this sort of software you generally start out with the simplest functions that initialize and read and write the registers. Once you have something that works you move on to refactor this into a suitable class. This is what happened in this case, but I'm only going to present the final, slightly polished, class.

First we need to initialize the SPI bus correctly:

```
class DS3234rtc(SPIDevice):
    def __init__(self):
        super(DS3234rtc, self).__init__()
        self.clock_mode=1
        self.select_high=False
        self._spi._interface.max_speed_hz=5000000
```

Notice that if you are using software SPI, you need to reduce the frequency of the clock.

Next we need a method to set each register of the clock device to the current time. Python has a `datetime` class that will store a complete date and time and can be used to get the current date/time. It has nearly all the information we need to set the DS3234, but in the wrong format. The idea is to use the `datetime` class to construct a tuple which has the information in the same order as the registers:

```
(seconds,minutes,hours,day,date, month,year)
```

The Python `datetime` object has all of these except for `day` so we have to add it to the tuple.

First we convert the `datetime` object to a tuple:

```
datetimetuple=dateTime.timetuple()
```

This gives us a tuple in the following format:

```
(year,month,date,hours,minutes,seconds)
```

We can add the day using the `isoweekday` method and we also need to change the year date to just the last two digits, i.e. subtract 2000:

```
datetimetuple=(datetimetuple[0]-2000,)+datetimetuple[1:3]+
              (dateTime.isoweekday(),)+datetimetuple[3:6]
```

Now we have a tuple that contains all the data, but in reverse order. The solution is to reverse it:

```
datetimetuple=datetimetuple[::-1]
```

With the data in the right format we can now write it to the device:

```
for i in range(0,7):
        data=datetimetuple[i]
        data=(data//10)<<4 |(data%10)
        words=self._spi.transfer([0x80+i,data])
```

The only complicated part is the instruction:

```
data=(data//10)<<4 |(data%10)
```

which performs binary to BCD conversion. The easiest way to understand this is via an example. If data is 59 then integer division by ten, i.e. `data//10`, gives 5 or `0101` in binary. A left shift by four, i.e. `<<4`, gives `01010000`. The remainder on division by 10, i.e. `data%10`, gives 9 or `1001` and OR-ing this with the previous result gives `01011001`, which is the BCD representation of 59, i.e. binary 5 in the high four bits and binary 9 in the low order bits.

We also need a method to read the data back from the device and this uses the same techniques to convert the BCD to binary and then construct a List with everything in the correct order. The List is then used to create a datetime object:

```
def getDateTime(self):
    datetimelist=[]
    for i in range(7):
        words=self._spi.transfer([i,0x00])
        if i==3:continue
        byte=words[1]
        data=(byte & 0x0F)+(byte>>4)*10
        datetimelist.insert(0,data)
    datetimelist[0]+=2000
    return datetime(*datetimelist)
```

The if statement omits the day register from the List as it isn't used in a datetime object. The List is constructed by inserting each item at its start, automatically producing it in the reverse order.

Putting all this together gives:

```python
class DS3234rtc(SPIDevice):
    def __init__(self):
        super(DS3234rtc, self).__init__()
        self.clock_mode=1
        self.select_high=False
        self._spi._interface.max_speed_hz=5000000

    def setDateTime(self,dateTime):
        datetimetuple=dateTime.timetuple()
        datetimetuple=(datetimetuple[0]-2000,)+datetimetuple[1:3]+
                      (dateTime.isoweekday(),+datetimetuple[3:6]
        datetimetuple=datetimetuple[::-1]
        for i in range(0,7):
            data=datetimetuple[i]
            data=(data//10)<<4 |(data%10)
            words=self._spi.transfer([0x80+i,data])


    def getDateTime(self):
        datetimelist=[]
        for i in range(7):
            words=self._spi.transfer([i,0x00])
            if i==3:continue
            byte=words[1]
            data=(byte & 0x0F)+(byte>>4)*10
            datetimelist.insert(0,data)
        datetimelist[0]+=2000
        return datetime(*datetimelist)
```

As an example of using it, the following program sets the date and time and then prints the date and time every few seconds:

```python
rtc=DS3234rtc()
rtc.setDateTime(datetime.today())
while True:
    t=rtc.getDateTime()
    print(t)
    sleep(1)
```

You can create custom classes for other SPI devices. The steps are always the same – identify the SPI connections and modes and then work out what registers you need to read and write to work with it. For complex devices this can seem like a large task and can be difficult to get right. Always try the simplest thing you can do to get started.

Summary

- Unlike other serial buses, the SPI makes use of unidirectional connections.

- The data lines are MOSI (master output slave input) and MISO (master input slave output).

- In addition, there is a clock line, output from master, and a number of select lines, two in the case of the Pi.

- Data is transferred from the master to the slave and from the slave to the master on each clock pulse, arranged as a circular buffer.

- You can test the SPI bus using a simple loopback connection.

- Working with a single slave is usually fairly easy, working with multiple slaves can be more of a problem.

- Making SPI work with any particular device has four steps:

  i.   Discover how to connect the device to the SPI pins. This is a matter of identifying pinouts and mostly what chip selects are supported.

  ii. Find out how to configure the Pi's SPI bus to work with the device. This is mostly a matter of clock speed and mode.

  iii. Identify the commands that you need to send to the device to get it to do something and what data it sends back as a response.

  iv. Find, or work out, the relationship between the raw reading, the voltage and the quantity the voltage represents.

- Implementing any custom device using almost any method of connection generally involves a great deal of bit manipulation.

Chapter 15

Using The Lgpio Library

Although this book is about GPIO Zero, the default pin factory that it uses is based on the lgpio library which provides a lower level way of working with the hardware. lgpio is a Python library that uses the Linux GPIO and other drivers to access the hardware. It lacks any object-oriented features and as such is potentially faster and not as abstract. If GPIO Zero is two steps away from the hardware, lgpio is at only one remove. What this means is that you can use it to do things that aren't implemented in GPIO Zero and you can use its functions to implement objects that do the same job and so extend GPIO Zero in new ways that are still reasonably machine-independent.

lgpio is a large collection of functions and covering them all would take a book in its own right. This chapter explains the basic philosophy and organization of the library and the principles you need to know to make good use of it.

A First Program Blinky

You don't need to do anything new to use lgpio as you have already been using it as the pin factory for GPIO Zero. Even if you haven't, the library is installed by default on all Pis – you simply have to import it. The Linux drivers that lgpio makes use of all follow the same basic idea. They convert the hardware in question to things that look like files. For example, the Linux GPIO driver makes the GPIO hardware look like folders in the file system. If you look in the /dev directory you will find files corresponding to each GPIO controller installed. You will see at least:

/dev/gpiochip0

This represents the main GPIO controller and all of the GPIO lines it provides. On the Pi 5 this is represented by:

/dev/gpiochip4

and this is a small by irritating difference that means your programs have to be slightly different to work on a Pi 5.

To work with the drivers you basically have to treat them as files and read and write data from and to them. lgpio does this for you and this allows you to use the drivers by making function calls to the library. For example to implement a Blinky program all you have to do is open a GPIO chip, claim a line to use as output and start writing data to it:

```
import lgpio

GPIOChip = lgpio.gpiochip_open(0)

lgpio.gpio_claim_output(GPIOChip, 4)

while True:
    lgpio.gpio_write(GPIOChip, 4, 0)
    lgpio.gpio_write(GPIOChip, 4, 1)

lgpio.gpiochip_close(GPIOChip)
```

The first instruction opens the "chip" that operates the GPIO lines we are trying to use. There can be more than one chip and some offer GPIO lines you can use and some are only for internal use. On the Pi 5 the chip is gpiochip4 and on all others it is gpiochip0. If you plan to run this program on a Pi 5 change:

```
GPIOChip = lgpio.gpiochip_open(0)
```

to:

```
GPIOChip = lgpio.gpiochip_open(4)
```

The open returns a reference to the open chip that you have to use in other function calls. The claim_output function sets the specified GPIO line, GPIO4 in this case, to be an output and "claims" it in the sense that another program using the GPIO lines via the driver cannot make use of it. The while loop simply sets the specified GPIO line, 4 in this case, to 0 and 1 alternately. Although the close function is never called, you should close a GPIO chip when you are finished with it – this releases all of the claimed GPIO lines so that other programs can use them.

If you run this on a Pi 5 you will find that the pulses about 1.5μs. A Pi 4 is slightly faster at 1μs and a Pi Zero 2W is slower at 2μs. However, this is still ten times faster than using GPIO Zero and a raw Pin object.

Basic GPIO Functions

The basic GPIO functions concerned with opening and closing a particular GPIO chip are:

- gpiochip_open   Opens a GPIO chip
- gpiochip_close   Closes a GPIO chip

You have to open a GPIO chip before you can work with any GPIO lines and you should close it when finished. Other programs can open a GPIO chip while you have it open and make use of it, but they cannot use any GPIO lines you have claimed unless you release them, see the line functions later, or close the chip.

You can find out the basic information about a GPIO chip using:

◆ gpio_get_chip_info   Gets information about a GPIO chip

This returns a list with a range of information, including what lines the chip supports. In most cases you write programs that assume a basic chip configuration and this function is really only useful for exploring a new machine.

In most cases you open a GPIO chip to make use of its GPIO lines. You can find out about a particular line using:

◆ gpio_get_line_info   Gets information about a GPIO line

◆ gpio_get_mode   Gets the mode of a GPIO line

The mode is a number that tells you if the line is input or output and what is using it. See the documentation for a table of results.

Before you can use a GPIO line you have to claim it. There are three functions that can claim a line for input, output and alert:

◆ gpio_claim_input   Claims a GPIO for input

◆ gpio_claim_output   Claims a GPIO for output

◆ gpio_claim_alert   Claims a GPIO for alerts

The line can also be configured using the lflags parameter which can be set to any of:

```
SET_ACTIVE_LOW
SET_OPEN_DRAIN
SET_OPEN_SOURCE
SET_PULL_UP
SET_PULL_DOWN
SET_PULL_NONE
```

Claiming a line for an alert makes it an input that will set an event according to how the eFlags parameter is set:

```
RISING_EDGE
FALLING_EDGE
BOTH_EDGES
```

Once you have claimed a GPIO line you can use:

◆ gpio_read   Reads a GPIO line

◆ gpio_write   Writes a GPIO line

◆ gpio_free   Frees a GPIO

As another simple example, consider setting two lines out of phase:

```
import lgpio

GPIOChip = lgpio.gpiochip_open(4)

lgpio.gpio_claim_output(GPIOChip, 4)
lgpio.gpio_claim_output(GPIOChip, 17)
while True:
    lgpio.gpio_write(GPIOChip, 4, 1)
    lgpio.gpio_write(GPIOChip, 17, 0)
    lgpio.gpio_write(GPIOChip, 4, 0)
    lgpio.gpio_write(GPIOChip, 17, 1)
lgpio.gpiochip_close(GPIOChip)
```

If you try this out on a Pi 5 you will find the pulses are $4\mu s$ and there is a $2\mu s$ lag in changing state:

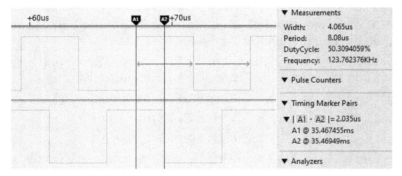

Group GPIO

As well as single line operations you can work with groups of lines:

- ◆ group_claim_input   Claims a group of GPIO lines for inputs
- ◆ group_claim_output   Claims a group of GPIO lines for outputs
- ◆ group_free   Frees a group of GPIO lines
- ◆ group_read   Reads a group of GPIO lines
- ◆ group_write   Writes a group of GPIO lines

In each case the function accepts a list of lines to claim. The first specified GPIO line is used as the name of the group. For example, [4,17] specifies GPIO4 and GPIO17 and from this point on the group is referenced by 4. The state of the GPIO group is represented by a binary value with each line represented by the corresponding bit. So the GPIO group [4,17] is represented by a two-bit number, 00 if both lines are low, 01 if GPIO4 is low and GPIO17 is high, 10 if GPIO4 is high and GPIO17 is low and 11 if both lines are high. You can also specify a `group_mask` which has a `1` where the line is to be changed and `0` where a line is not to be altered.

So for example:

```
lgpio.group_claim_output(GPIOChip, [4,17])
```

claims lines GPIO4 and GPIO17 as an output group.

To write to the groups you would use:

```
lgpio.group_write(GPIOChip, 4, 2)
```

The `4` identifies the group using the lead GPIO line. The 2 specifies the binary value `10` which sets GPIO4 high and GPIO17 low.

You can use the group functions to implement a phased output:

```
import lgpio

GPIOChip = lgpio.gpiochip_open(4)

lgpio.group_claim_output(GPIOChip, [4,17])

while True:
    lgpio.group_write(GPIOChip, 4, 2)
    lgpio.group_write(GPIOChip, 4, 1)
```

This sets the group of lines GPIO4 and GPIO17 to `10` and then `01`. If you try this out you will find that the pulses are fast, but there is still a small lag between the lines being set. For a Pi 5 the pulses are 1.5μs and the lag is less than 0.1us, which is much better than switching the lines independently.

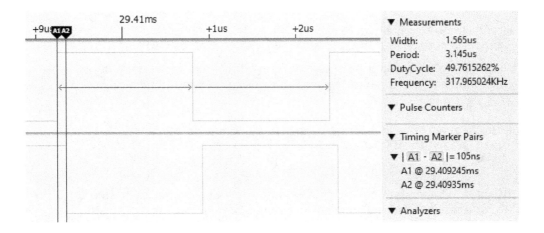

227

The Pulses

Once you have a GPIO line you can use it to create pulses of any duration you care to implement. The lgpio library has done some of the work for you by providing a set of functions that will pulse a GPIO line in a particular way. Notice that all of these pulses are generated in software. For example,

```
tx_pwm(handle, gpio, pwm_frequency, pwm_duty_cycle,
                        pulse_offset=0, pulse_cycles=0)
```

This starts software timed PWM on an output GPIO and has the parameters:

- ◆ `handle`   As returned by `gpiochip_open`
- ◆ `gpio`   GPIO line to be pulsed
- ◆ `pwm_frequency`   PWM frequency in Hz (0=off, `0.1-10000`).
- ◆ `pwm_duty_cycle` PWM duty cycle in % (0-100).
- ◆ `pulse_offset`   Offset from nominal pulse start position.
- ◆ `pulse_cycles`   Number of cycles to be sent, 0 for infinite.

So, for example, to send 50 pulses at 1000Hz with a 25% duty cycle using GPIO4 you would use;

```
lgpio.tx_pwm(GPIOChip, 4, 1000, 25,pulse_cycles=50)
```

There is no need to claim the GPIO line as it is automatically claimed and set to output. The PWM is generated in software rather than making any use of the Pi's PWM hardware. An interrupt routine is used to generate the pulses and this only runs while the program is running. If you try:

```
import lgpio

GPIOChip = lgpio.gpiochip_open(4)
lgpio.tx_pwm(GPIOChip, 4, 1000, 25,pulse_cycles=50)
```

then you won't see any pulses output on GPIO4 as the program ends before they start being generated. To see the pulses you need to use:

```
import lgpio

GPIOChip = lgpio.gpiochip_open(4)
lgpio.tx_pwm(GPIOChip, 4, 1000, 25,pulse_cycles=50)
while True:
    pass
```

If you don't specify a `pulse_cycles` then the waveform is generated until the program ends. You can modify the waveform being produced by simply using another `tx_pwm` function call.

For example:

```
import lgpio
import time

GPIOChip = lgpio.gpiochip_open(4)
lgpio.tx_pwm(GPIOChip, 4, 1000, 25)
time.sleep(1)
lgpio.tx_pwm(GPIOChip, 4, 1000, 50)
while True:
    pass
```

This starts the pulse generator at 1000Hz with a 25% duty cycle and then after one second changes this to 50% duty cycle.

The important idea is that the pulse generator maintains a queue of pulse instructions. Each pulse function call takes a single slot in the queue and as one function call comes to an end, the next one in the queue is started. The pulse function returns the number of free spaces in the queue and you can check to see how many slots are free using:

```
tx_room(handle, gpio, kind)
```

where kind is TX_PWM or TX_WAVE.

For example:

```
import lgpio

GPIOChip = lgpio.gpiochip_open(4)
lgpio.tx_pwm(GPIOChip, 4, 1000, 25,pulse_cycles=100)
lgpio.tx_pwm(GPIOChip, 4, 1000, 50,pulse_cycles=100)
while True:
    pass
```

In this case the first function call adds one item to the queue for 100 cycles of 1000Hz, 25% duty cycle and the second call adds another item to the queue for 100 cycles of 1000Hz with a 50% duty cycle. As before, the program has to carry on running for all of the items in the queue to be processed.

Even though you can, in theory, set the frequency to 10kHz, this is not a good idea. Even at 1kHz the pulse generator is interrupted by the operating system often enough to be a nuisance:

When the pulse generator is restarted it generates pulses with a shorter period to catch up with the pulse stream. As a result you cannot rely on the pulse time or the duty cycle. The amount of irregularity depends on the loading of the processor.

As well as specifying frequency and duty cycle, you can specify the time the pulse is high and low:

```
tx_pulse(handle, gpio, pulse_on, pulse_off,
                          pulse_offset=0, pulse_cycles=0)
```

where the pulse on and off times are in microseconds. For example:

```
lgpio.tx_pulse(GPIOChip,4,pulse_on=100,pulse_off=100)
```

generates a pulse train at 5kHz with a 50% duty cycle. This uses the same pulse generator and queue as the PWM function.

As PWM is used to control servos, it makes sense to have a special servo related function:

```
tx_servo(handle, gpio, pulse_width, servo_frequency=50,
                          pulse_offset=0, pulse_cycles=0)
```

You can generally ignore the servo_frequency as it is usually 50Hz. The pulse_width varies from $500\mu s$ to $2500\mu s$, which is the range needed to take a servo from its extreme positions. In practice you would have to calibrate the servo to discover the exact range to use. For example:

```
lgpio.tx_servo(GPIOChip, 4, 500)
```

sets a servo connected to GPIO4 to one of its two extreme positions.

This is simple, but the inaccuracies in the pulse stream referred to in the discussion of PWM now become more of a problem. The documentation says:

> *The timing jitter will cause the servo to fidget. This may cause it to overheat and wear out prematurely.*

In most cases the jitter is small enough not to be a worry except for long-term use.

Finally we have

```
tx_wave(handle, gpio, pulses)
```

which can be used to pulse a set of GPIO lines in a complex pattern.

The gpio parameter is a group of GPIO lines and pulses is a list of pulse objects.

A pulse object is a container class with the following members:

- group_bits   Levels to set if the corresponding bit in group_mask is set
- group_mask   Mask indicating the group GPIO to be updated
- pulse_delay   Delay in microseconds before the next pulse

This works like the PWM queue but using its own queue. You can check how much space there is using:

tx_room(handle, gpio, *kind*)

with *kind* set to TX_WAVE.

To pulse GPIO1 and GPIO17 out of phase you could use:

```
import lgpio
from collections import namedtuple

Pulse = namedtuple('Pulse', ['group_bits',
                               'group_mask', 'pulse_delay'])

GPIOChip = lgpio.gpiochip_open(4)
lgpio.group_claim_output(GPIOChip, [4,17])

lgpio.tx_wave(GPIOChip, 4,[Pulse(1,3,1000),Pulse(2,3,1000),
                            Pulse(1,3,1000),Pulse(2,3,1000)] )

while True:
    pass
```

In this we first define a named tuple suitable for storing a Pulse specification. Then we setup a GPIO group consisting of GPIO4 and GPIO17. The call to tw_wave changes both lines at the same time – the mask is 3 or 11 in binary. The first Pulse sets GPIO4 high and GPIO17 low for 1000μs. The second sets GPIO4 low and GPIO17 high for 1000μs and this is repeated once. If you run the program you will see:

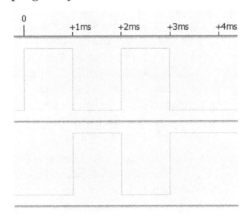

If you want to keep the pulse trains going then you need a loop to keep the queue filled:

```
import lgpio
from collections import namedtuple

Pulse = namedtuple('Pulse', ['group_bits', 'group_mask',
                                         'pulse_delay'])

GPIOChip = lgpio.gpiochip_open(4)
lgpio.group_claim_output(GPIOChip, [4,17])
while True:
    if lgpio.tx_room(GPIOChip,4,lgpio.TX_WAVE)>2:
        lgpio.tx_wave(GPIOChip, 4,
                [Pulse(1,3,1000),Pulse(2,3,1000)])
```

The if statement checks to see if there is enough room in the queue and then adds two Pulse specifications if there is. If you try this out you will find that you get a continuous phased pulse stream, but there are still irregularities:

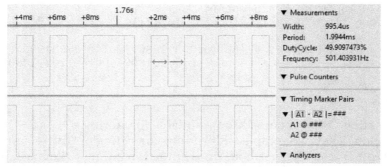

More lgpio

As well as the basic GPIO functions there are also functions to use the serial port, I2C and SPI buses. All three are implemented in hardware and make use of the corresponding Linux drivers for the device. This means that they should work without glitches but it also means that they are only as good as the Linux drivers. The drivers for the Pi family work well enough to make these functions attractive. GPIO Zero has an SPI object and this makes it a better choice for this bus. However it doesn't provide an object for the I2C or serial interfaces. If you are interested in using either then the raw Linux drivers are not difficult to use and you can find out more in *Raspberry Pi IOT in Python with Linux Drivers, 2nd Ed*, ISBN:9781871962864.

The lgpio functions are also not difficult but they are beyond the scope of this book. If you find that you are contemplating making use of them, it may well be a sign that you have outgrown GPIO Zero.

Summary

- The GPIO Zero library is based on using the lgpio library as its pin factory for all versions of the Pi.

- The lgpio library is installed by default alongside GPIO Zero and as such it is tempting to use it directly to increase speed and access missing features.

- The lgpio library makes use of Linux GPIO drivers and as such is slower than direct access to the hardware, but has the advantage of being largely hardware independent.

- Linux drivers are used as if they were files and data is transferred using read and write operations. The lgpio library deals with this lower level interaction for you and provides functions to deal with the drivers.

- For a Pi 5 the GPIO driver file name is `gpiochip4` and for all other Pis it is `gpiochip0`. This is the only difference in using `lgpio` with the Pi 5.

- Before you can use GPIO lines you have to open the GPIO driver and remember to close it again when you are finished using the line.

- Functions are provided to let you configure and use GPIO line objects.

- There are also functions that work with groups of GPIO line objects.

- For more sophisticated output you can use the pulse functions which generate preset pulse trains from one or more GPIO lines.

- The most useful of the pulse functions are the PWM function and the servo function.

- There are also functions that use GPIO lines to work with serial, I2C and SPI buses.

Appendix I
VS Code

Microsoft's Visual Studio Code, VS Code, has good Python support, runs on a range of platforms including the Raspberry Pi and is possibly a better choice of code editor than Thonny, as it has full remote Python development including debugging. That is, you can write your program on a desktop, generally a more powerful machine, and run it on a Pi connected over SSH and single step and breakpoint it.

The only problem with this approach is that VS Code has more facilities than you need to just run Python, it supports a wide range of languages, and this can make it confusing. However, after you have run your first program, it all becomes so much easier. If you are going to be doing much programming on Pis, this is worth the effort in setting up and mastering it.

As it is under constant development, it is probably better to consult its website to find the latest instructions on how to install it and its various components.

VS Code doesn't support remote working on the Pi Zero and Zero W. This presents a problem as the device you most want to remote operate with is the Pi Zero/W. Even though it works on a Pi Zero 2W, the lack of memory makes it slow. It also approaches the problem of remote working in a way that is less useful for IoT applications. It keeps all of the programs on the remote device. which makes managing code more difficult than if the code is kept on the local device.

A more useful, but slightly more complicated, approach is to make use of VS Code Tasks to provide remote build and debug. This works with all versions of the Pi, or indeed any Linux-based device, and it keeps all of the files on the local machine. It also works with the Pi Zero/W and is described later.

SSH Without a Password

Before trying to make any of the following work, you need to have set up SSH access using a key file. Some of the commands work if you simply supply a password, but the debugging commands don't.

Using a password to connect over SSH is fine when you are just testing the installation, but the number of times you are asked to provide it quickly becomes irritating. The solution is to create a key pair to use. If you look up the instructions for doing this, you might conclude that it is very difficult. This is because every effort is make to ensure security is enforced. If you simply want to use a key as a way of avoiding having to supply a password then you can take shortcuts. As long as you keep your private key safe, the setup is secure.

The first step is generating a key pair on the local machine. As long as you have OpenSSH installed, this is easy. The steps described here will work on Windows, Mac and Linux. If you are using Windows, start a PowerShell session:

```
cd ~\.ssh
ssh-keygen -t rsa
```

This generates a default RSA key in the .ssh directory within the current user's home directory. You can provide a name for the key files and in this example the name pi is used, although this doesn't affect what device you can use them for. There are advantages in using the default name.

You will see output something like:

```
Generating public/private rsa key pair.
Enter file in which to save the key (C:\Users\
userhome/.ssh/id_rsa): pi
Enter passphrase (empty for no passphrase):
Enter same passphrase again:
Your identification has been saved in pi.
Your public key has been saved in pi.pub.
The key fingerprint is:
SHA256:UtiQ3RMYpluJb+nx8n5pqsbLXHgiYv2hKs1EVoF7vqQ user@Rockrose
The key's randomart image is:
+---[RSA 2048]----+
|      .o+o+..     |
|     . oBo.o      |
|      o+ =  .     |
|     + .= .       |
|    o oo S        |
|     ..o+ +       |
|    +oooo* +  .   |
|    ..E..*oB  +   |
|    .....*+++     |
+----[SHA256]-----+
```

If you really are using the keys for security purposes you should supply a passphrase, which is requested when the key pair is used. If you are simply using the keys to avoid entering a password then leave the passphrase blank for simplicity.

The key generation will leave two files in the .ssh directory – in this case pi and pi.pub. The first is the private key and this you keep to yourself as it is what proves that the machine is the one that the public key belongs to. The pi.pub file contains the public key and this is the one that has to be copied to the remote machine. The remote machine uses the public key to challenge the local machine to decode something which can only be done with the private key, so proving that the machine is legitimate, or rather that it has the private key.

You can use the public key with as many remote machines as you need to. The key identifies you as being allowed to connect to a machine that has it using SSH. To make this happen, you have to enter the details of the file into .ssh/authorized_keys. You can do this any way you know how to, but the public key file has to be copied to ~/.ssh/ on the remote machine and renamed authorized_keys. As you have SSH working, the simplest thing to do is:

```
scp pi.pub pi@192.168.11.151:~/.ssh/authorized_keys
```

You might have to make the .ssh folder first. You will have to provide the user's password. If this works you will find authorized_keys in the .ssh directory. If you want to store more public keys in authorized_keys so that more than one user can log on, you have to append additional public key files to authorized_keys.

SSH will not use the key file if ~/.ssh or ~ are writable by Group or Others. One way of ensuring this is not the case:

```
chmod 700 ~/.ssh
chmod 600 ~/.ssh/authorized_keys
```

As long as the permissions are set correctly, you should be able to connect without a password using:

```
ssh -i ~/.ssh/pi pi@192.168.11.151
```

If you don't use -i ~/.ssh/pi to specify the private key file, you might be asked for a password as well as the key file. You also have to specify the correct user name.

If you want to log on and not specify the key file, i.e. just using:

```
pi@192.168.11.151
```

then you need to make sure your key files have the correct default names. For protocol 2 the keys have to be called id_rsa and id_rsa.pub. If you use these default names for RSA keys then the SSH agent will use them automatically. If you use any other names, like pi and pi.pub, you will need an Identity file specified in .ssh config.

Open the file config in the C:\Users\user\.ssh directory on the local machine (~/.ssh under Linux) and enter:

```
Host 192.168.11.151
    HostName 192.168.11.151
    User pi
    PubKeyAuthentication yes
    IdentityFile ~/.ssh/pi
```

Of course, you have to change the IP address, user name and the location of the key file to be correct for the machine you are trying to connect to. You can enter additional Host specifications for each machine you want to connect to.

After this you should be able to connect and work with the remote Pi without providing a password when using VS Code. You can also just use:

```
ssh pi@192.168.11.151
```

at the command line.

Notice that this is low security as we didn't specify a passphrase to use with the private key. If you need security from the outside world, you need to create a key with a passphrase and then you need to use the SSH agent to supply it automatically.

Remote Python With VS Code

The easiest way to implement remote development is to use the standard remote development add-ins for VS Code on a desktop machine. The programs you develop are stored on the remote machine, but you can work with them as if they were on the desktop machine. Ideally, you would like to keep the programs on the desktop machine and automatically download to the remote machine as required and this is what the alternative approach using VS Code tasks does, see later. Notice that VS Code remote development add-ins do not work on a Pi Zero, but the VS Code tasks work on all Pis.

First install the up-to-date stable version of VS Code appropriate for the platform you are using from the VS Code website. It works under Windows, Debian and Mac OS. You can also find versions for other operating systems, but usually without installers.

Once you have VS Code installed to run Python programs you first need to install the Microsoft Python extension which automatically installs Pylance:

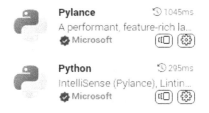

To run the remote development extension you need to have an OpenSSH client running on the development machine. Windows has its own version of OpenSSH client. You next need to install the remote development pack. You only need to install Remote SSH.

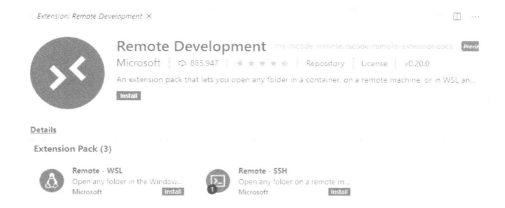

After you have installed Remote SSH you can add the details of the Pi you want to use to develop programs on. To do this click on the Remote Explorer icon in the left panel and you will see that there are no SSH clients installed.

Next click on the + that appears when you hover over SSH Targets and enter the details for the Pi you want to connect to:

You specify the host using the format:

```
ssh user@ipaddress
```

When you press Enter, select a configuration file to use and you are ready to connect to the new host. Right-click on the new host and select Connect in this window. Next, you will be asked for your password. You will be asked for the password each time you connect unless you create a private key and use it for authentication as detailed earlier.

When you open the File Explorer and select Open Folder you will see a list of folders stored in your home folder on the host machine. Create a new folder suitable for storing your Python programs and create a file called Hello.py in it. The new file will open in the editor and you can type in:

```
print("Hello World")
```

Next select Run, Run Without Debugging and select the Current Python file if asked for the run configuration. You will be prompted to install Python extensions on the remote machine and to select a Python interpreter to use. As long as you do this you should see Hello World appear in the console at the bottom of the window. This program has been run on the remote machine. From here on you can learn about VS Code and slowly customize it to make your work easier.

Running With Root Permissions

IoT programs often need root permissions to access hardware. The simplest way to do this is to run the program locally using `sudo`. A better way if you want to debug your program is to create a `launch.json` file:

```
{
    "version": "0.2.0",
    "configurations": [
        {
            "name": "Sudo Python: Current File",
            "type": "python",
            "request": "launch",
            "program": "${file}",
            "console": "integratedTerminal",
            "justMyCode": true,
            "sudo": true
        }
    ]
}
```

Notice the "sudo":true at the end. This runs the Python interpreter using sudo. This only works for Python programs. You now have to run the debug using the RUN menu.

Local Remote Synchronization

It is important to realize that the Python programs you create are stored on the remote host. This means that, if you do nothing about it, your entire program could be stored solely on a Pi, waiting for something bad to happen to it. Even if you consider this a safe option, you have the problem of transferring the program to another Pi if you want to run it there. The best solution is to keep a copy of your programs on a machine that you consider safe, and share them with any Pi you might want to run them on.

The most attractive option is to use source code management. VS Code supports Git without you having to install any extensions. Once you have it all set up this works well, but setting it up is a time-consuming process and it requires that you understand how Git, and usually GitHub, works. For small and simple projects this is generally more than you need and you could spend a lot of valuable programming time learning to use a tool that you barely make use of. This said, if you are planning a large project, or a collaborative project, then source code management is your best option, even if it does involve additional initial work.

In most cases we can achieve what we need using simpler tools. You can copy a single file or folder from a remote machine by drag-and-dropping it from the File Explorer to the folder in the local machine. Unfortunately, this doesn't work for remote Linux machines, and this includes Pi OS, so it isn't a method that works for us. However, you can drag-and-drop files and folders from the local machine to the File Explorer window on the remote machine. See the next section for an automatic way of doing this.

Now we only have the problem of copying files from the remote machine to the local machine. This can be done by selecting a file or folder in the VS Code File Explorer and right-clicking to display the context menu. You will see Download in the same section as Copy. Selecting this downloads the entire folder and its contents or the single file. You can pick where you want the file or folder to be copied to and so manually maintain a central copy of anything you are working on.

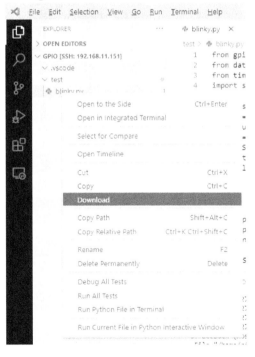

An alternative way of saving a remote file on the local machine is to use the File, Save As menu option and select the Show Local button.

This allows you to save the file on the local machine under whatever name you want to use.

There are ways of automating the copying of files, but manual copying works well and most of the automatic synchronizing methods have their own drawbacks.

VS Code Remote Build and Debug Tasks

An alternative to using VS Code's own remote development facilities is to use custom tasks to copy and compile the program on the remote machine. This has the advantage that it works on all versions of the Pi and you automatically keep the source of all of the programs on the local machine.

If you just want to use the tasks for remote debugging or remote running of a Python program using VS Code then the steps are given below. The files used have been tested on Windows, but they should work on Mac OS and Linux with changes to the folders specified. The files are listed at the end of this appendix and you can download them from this book's page on www.iopress.info.

It is important to know that you need to set up SSH connections without a password for many of these steps to work and you might need to login as root for some of the programs to work.

Create the folder that is going to act as the project folder for all of the Python programs you are going to work with. In this case it is called GPIOZERO, but there is nothing special about this name. The directory structure is important to the working of the tasks as they assume that VS Code has the top-level directory, i.e. GPIOZERO, open, even though you are working with files in HelloWorld

Create the .vscode folder in the top-level of the folder. Again, it is important that you create the folder in GPIOZERO as the configuration files apply to all of the subdirectories.

Create a test project folder HelloWorld in this case and create a simple Hello.py test program.

Download the three files settings.json, tasks.json and launch.json from the I/O Press website, www.iopress.info, or type them in from the listings at the end of this appendix, and copy them into the .vscode folder.

Edit settings.json in the .vscode folder to read something like:

```
{
    "sshUser": "pi",
    "sshEndpoint": "192.168.11.170",
    "remoteDirectory": "/home/pi/Documents/",
}
```

Change the user name, IP address and the directory you want to use to store your programs in.

If you haven't already done so, you need to install debugpy, which is the latest Python debugger for VS Code. On the remote machine, i.e. the Pi, enter:

```
python3 -m pip install debugpy
```

If you don't have a virtual environment set up you may need to use:

```
python3 -m pip install debugpy --break-system-packages
```

You have to do this on any machine you want to remote debug on.

To run a program, view the program in the editor and use the menu option Terminal,Run Build Task or press Ctrl+Shift+B. You will see the program files being copied and then you will see the output of the program in the terminal window. Notice that you will not see any graphics and you can't provide input to the program. For general-purpose Python programs this would be a problem, but for IoT programs it usually isn't. Notice that if you have to provide a password for SSH connections you will be asked to supply it. Use the StopRemotePython task to stop all Python programs on the remote machine.

To debug a program, first use the menu option Terminal,Run Task and select tunnel. You will see a terminal open and connect to the remote computer. You only need to establish a tunnel once and you can check if one is already open by the presence of a terminal window labeled Task - tunnel. Don't try to open more than one tunnel and note that remote debugging won't work unless you have a tunnel to the remote machine open.

You also need to make sure that the workspace folder is present on the remote machine. You can use the makeRemoteWorkSpace task to do this.

The Task Files

Both of the following files are created in the .vscode folder in the top level of the folder that you open in VS Code.

settings.json

This file has to be customized to your IP, user name and folder:

```
{
    "sshUser": "pi",
    "sshEndpoint": "192.168.11.151",
    "remoteDirectory": "/home/pi/Documents/",

}
```

tasks.json

```
{
    "version": "2.0.0",
    "tasks": [
        {
            "label": "copyToRemote",
            "type": "shell",
            "command": "scp -r ${fileDirname}
                ${config:sshUser}@${config:sshEndpoint}:
                    ${config:remoteDirectory}/",
            "problemMatcher": [],
            "presentation": {
                "showReuseMessage": false,
                "clear": true
            }
        },

        {
            "label": "makeRemoteWorkSpace",
            "type": "shell",
            "command": "ssh ${config:sshUser}@${config:sshEndpoint}
                    'mkdir  ${config:remoteDirectory}'",
            "problemMatcher": [],
            "presentation": {
                "showReuseMessage": false,
            }
        },
        {
            "label": "RunR",
            "type": "shell",
            "command": "ssh ${config:sshUser}@${config:sshEndpoint}
                'python3 ${config:remoteDirectory}
                    ${relativeFileDirname}/${fileBasename}'",
            "problemMatcher": [],
            "presentation": {
                "showReuseMessage": false,
```

```
        }
    },
    {
        "label": "RunRemote",
        "dependsOrder": "sequence",
        "dependsOn": [
            "copyToRemote",
            "RunR"
        ],
        "problemMatcher": [],
        "group": {
            "kind": "build",
            "isDefault": true
        },
    },

    {
        "label": "StopREmotePython",
        "type": "shell",
        "command": "ssh ${config:sshUser}@${config:sshEndpoint}
                                        'pkill python3'",
        "problemMatcher": [],
        "presentation": {
            "showReuseMessage": true,
        }
    },
    {
        "label": "wait",
        "type": "shell",
        "command": "timeout 10"
    },
```

```json
{
    "label": "tunnel",
    "type": "shell",
    "command": "ssh -2 -L 5678:localhost:5678
            ${config:sshUser}@${config:sshEndpoint}",
    "problemMatcher": [],
    "presentation": {
        "showReuseMessage": false,
    }
},
{

    "label": "startDebug",
    "type": "shell",
    "command":"ssh -2 ${config:sshUser}@
                            ${config:sshEndpoint}
      'nohup python3 -m debugpy --listen 0.0.0.0:5678
          --wait-for-client
    ${config:remoteDirectory}${relativeFileDirname}/
            ${fileBasename} > /dev/null 2>&1 &'",
    "problemMatcher": [],
    "presentation": {
        "showReuseMessage": false,
    }
},
{

    "label": "copyAndDebug",
    "dependsOrder": "sequence",
    "dependsOn": [
        "copyToRemote",
        "startDebug",
        "wait"
    ],
    "presentation": {
        "showReuseMessage": false,
    },
},
    ]
}
```

To summarize the tasks defined in `tasks.json`:

◆   copyToRemote

    Copies the current local directory to the remote machine. For example, if you have `hello.py` open in the editor and it is stored in the HelloWorld directory then running this task copies everything in HelloWorld on the local machine to the same directory on the remote machine.

◆   makeRemoteWorkSpace

    Creates the top level project directory on the remote machine. If the local machine's top level project directory is `GPIO` then running this task creates `/home/pi/Documents/GPIO`.

◆   RunR

    Runs the current program on the remote machine. If the current program in the editor is `hello.py` then running this task runs `hello.py` on the remote machine. It doesn't copy the files, for this use RunRemote.

◆   RunRemote

    Uploads the current directory and runs the current Python program. Equivalent to `copyToRemote` followed by `RunR`.

◆   StopRemotePython

    Stops all Python programs running on the remote machine.

◆   Wait

    Implements a 10-second wait. Used internally by `copyAndDebug` to allow time for the debugger to start.

◆   startDebug

    Starts the current program running on the remote under a debugger. Used internally.

◆   copyAndDebug

    Uses `copyToRemote` to copy the current folder to the remote machine and then uses `startDebug` to debug the program. Used internally.

Launch and Debug

To make use of remote debugging you need to install `debugpy`, which is the latest Python debugger for VS Code. On the remote machine, i.e. the Pi, enter:

```
python3 -m pip install debugpy
```

If you don't have a virtual environment set up you may need to use:

```
python3 -m pip install debugpy --break-system-packages
```

You also need a launch.json file in .vscode:

```json
{
    "version": "0.2.0",
    "configurations": [
        {
            "name": "Python: Remote Attach",
            "type": "python",
            "connect": {
                "host": "localhost",
                "port": 5678
            },
            "pathMappings": [
                {
                    "localRoot": "${workspaceFolder}/
                                  ${relativeFileDirname}/",
                    "remoteRoot": "${config:remoteDirectory}/
                                  ${relativeFileDirname}"
                }
            ],
            "request": "attach",
            "preLaunchTask": "copyAndDebug",
            "postDebugTask": "StopREmotePython"
        }
    ]
}
```

Index

Raspberry Pi IoT in Python With Linux Drivers, Second Edition
ISBN: 978-1871962864 (Paperback)
ISBN:978-1871962178 (Hardback)

If you opt to use Linux drivers to connect to external devices then Python becomes a good choice, as speed of execution is no longer a big issue. This book explains how to use Python to connect to and control external devices with the full current range of Raspberry Pis, including the Pi 5 and the Raspberry Pi Zero 2W using the standard Linux drivers.

Raspberry Pi IoT in C With Linux Drivers, Second Edition
ISBN: 978-1871962857 (Paperback)
ISBN: 978-1871962161 (Hardback)

This second edition has been updated and expanded to cover the Raspberry Pi 5 and the Raspberry Pi Zero W/2W. There are Linux drivers for many off-the-shelf IoT devices and they provide a very easy-to-use, high-level way of working. The big problem is that there is very little documentation to help you get started. This book explains the principles so that you can tackle new devices.

Raspberry Pi IoT in C, Third Edition
ISBN: 978-1871962840 (Paperback)
ISBN: 978-1871962154 (Hardback)

In this book you will find a practical approach to understanding electronic circuits and datasheets and translating this to code, specifically using the C programming language. The main reason for choosing C is speed, a crucial factor when you are writing programs to communicate with the outside world. If you are familiar with another programming language, C shouldn't be hard to pick up. This third edition has been brought up-to-date and includes the Pi Zero 2W and the latest OS. An entire chapter is devoted to the Pi 5 and it is covered elsewhere in the book wherever possible.

Programmer's Python:
Everything is an Object, Second Edition
ISBN: 978-1871962741

This book, the first in the *Something Completely Different* series, sets out to explain the deeper logic in the approach that Python 3 takes to classes and objects. The subject is roughly speaking everything to do with the way Python implements objects. That is, in order of sophistication: metaclass, class, object, attribute, and all the other facilities such as functions, methods and "magic methods" that Python uses to make it all work.

Programmer's Python: Everything is Data
ISBN: 978-1871962598

Following the *Something Completely Different* philosophy, this book approaches data in a distinctly Pythonic way. What we have in Python are data objects that are very usable and very extensible. From the unlimited precision integers, referred to as bignums, through the choice of a list to play the role of the array, to the availability of the dictionary as a built-in data type, Python has powerful special features. Complete chapters are devoted on Boolean logic, dates and times, regular expressions, bit manipulation, files, pickle and using ctypes.

Programmer's Python: Async
ISBN: 978-1871962765

For many reasons modern Python programs have to be asynchronous. This book, part of the *Something Completely Different* set focuses on all things async. It not only covers the latest asyncio in depth, but has all you need to know about the many approaches to async that Python provides – threads, processes, locks, communications, subprocesses, futures, tasks, schedulers and, of course, asyncio. This is the book you need to understand all the options, tradeoffs and gotchas.

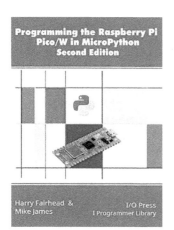

Programming the Raspberry Pi Pico/W in MicroPython, Second Edition
ISBN: 978-1871962802 (Paperback)
ISBN: 978-1871962062 (Hardback)

The Raspberry Pi Pico is a remarkable microcontroller. It has a power and sophistication that would have been unthinkable just a short time ago. Instead of struggling with the machine, you can now focus on a good implementation of your algorithms. The original version of this book, which covers getting the most from the Pico using MicroPython, predated the launch of the Wifi-enabled Pico W which is covered in this second edition.

Programming The Raspberry Pi Pico/W In C, Second Edition
ISBN: 978-1871962796 (Paperback)
ISBN: 978-1871962055 (Hardback)

This book explains the many reasons for wanting to use C with the Raspberry Pi Pico and Pico W, not least of which is the fact that it is much faster. This makes it ideal for serious experimentation and delving into parts of the hardware that are otherwise inaccessible. Using C is the way to get the maximum from the Pico and this book shows you how with many near-complete projects.

Master the Raspberry Pi Pico in C: WiFi
ISBN: 978-1871962819 (Paperback)
ISBN: 978-1871962079 (Hardback)

At a more advanced level, there is far too much to the Pico to cover in a single book and this follow-on title focuses on WiFi using the lwlp and mbedtls libraries to take your Pico C programming to the next level. For the Pico W it covers TLS/HTTPS connections, access point mode, other protocols and using FreeRTOS. Chapters are devoted to advanced hardware features such as DMA, watchdog timer and saving power.

Micro:bit IoT In C, Second Edition
ISBN: 978-1871962673

The second edition of this book covers V2, the revised version of the micro:bit. The other important change is that it now uses the highly popular VS Code for offline development and lets you get started the easy way by providing downloadable templates for both V1 and V2 of the micro:bit. The micro:bit lacks WiFi connectivity but using a low-cost device we enable a connection to the Internet via its serial port which allows it to become a server. The book rounds out with a new chapter on the micro:bit's radio and the V2's sound capabilities

Programming the ESP32 in MicroPython
ISBN: 978-1871962826(Paperback)
ISBN: 978-1871962093 (Hardback)

The ESP32 is a remarkable device. It is low cost, but with many different subsystems that make it more powerful than you might think. You can use it for simple applications because it is cheap, but you can also use it for more sophisticated applications because it is capable.

The purpose of the book is to reveal what you can do with the ESP's GPIO lines together with widely used sensors, servos and motors and ADCs. After covering the GPIO, outputs and inputs, events and interrupts, it gives you hands-on experience of PWM (Pulse Width Modulation), the SPI bus, the I2C bus and the 1-Wire bus. We also cover direct access to the hardware, adding an SD Card reader, sleep states to save power, the RTC, RMT and touch sensors, not to mention how to use WiFi.

www.ingramcontent.com/pod-product-compliance
Lightning Source LLC
LaVergne TN
LVHW062312060326
832902LV00013B/2167